The Work Trap

THE WORK TRAP

TED W. ENGSTROM
and
DAVID J. JUROE

Fleming H. Revell
Old Tappan, New Jersey

Unless otherwise identified, Scripture quotations are from the King James Version of the Bible.

Scripture quotations identified NAS are from the New American Standard Bible, Copyright © THE LOCKMAN FOUNDATION 1960, 1962, 1963, 1968, 1971, 1972, 1973, 1975 and are used by permission.

Scripture quotations identified PHILLIPS are from THE NEW TESTAMENT IN MODERN ENGLISH (Revised Edition), translated by J. B. Phillips. © J. B. Phillips 1958, 1960, 1972. Used by permission of Macmillan Publishing Co., Inc.

Scripture quotations identified RSV are from the Revised Standard Version of the Bible, copyrighted 1946, 1952, © 1971 and 1973.

Excerpts from *Freedom From Compulsion* by Leonard Cammer, M.D., copyright © 1976 by Harold I. Cammer and Robert Cammer, trustees FBO Beatrice Cammer. Reprinted by permission of SIMON & SCHUSTER, a Division of Gulf & Western Corporation.

Excerpts from LOVE AGAINST HATE by Karl Menninger published by Harcourt Brace Jovanovich, Inc., are reprinted by permission.

Excerpts from CONFESSIONS OF A WORKAHOLIC by Wayne Oates. Copyright © 1971 by Wayne Oates. Used by permission of Abingdon Press.

Excerpts from the book COMPASSION AND SELF-HATE by Dr. Theodore I. Rubin & Eleanor Rubin. Copyright © 1975 by El-Ted Rubin, Inc. Reprinted by permission of the David McKay Company, Inc.

Excerpts from "Confessions of a Workaholic" by C. Peter Wagner are reprinted by Permission of ETERNITY Magazine, Copyright 1975, Evangelical Ministries, 1716 Spruce Street, Philadelphia, PA 19103.

Excerpts from *Growing Toward Wholeness* by John Huffman, copyright © 1978, used by permission of Word Books, Publisher, Waco, Texas.

Material excerpted, by permission of the publisher, from *Anxiety and the Executive*, by Alan N. Schoonmaker © 1969 by American Management Association, Inc. All rights reserved.

Library of Congress Cataloging in Publication Data

Engstrom, Theodore Wilhelm, date
    The work trap.

    Bibliography: p.
    Includes index.
    1. Work—Psychological aspects. I. Juroe, David J., joint author. II. Title.
HF5548.8.E53   301.5'5   78-27656
ISBN 0-8007-0972-1

TO
Dorothy and Bonnie
who—more than anyone else—
have kept us out of the
Work Trap

Contents

8   CONTENTS

Introduction

"I CAN'T marry Jack—I just can't," Jean blurted out to her counselor, sobbing with heavy sighs. After a bit she was able to calm down, and continued, "All Jack does is stay at his desk and in his office day and night, night and day. That man might as well be tied with a rope to his desk. He won't budge. He claims he loves me, but I swear, he's married to his job and I come second, always. I know it's not necessary that he work such long hours . . . he must dawdle or something. I can't even get him to take me anywhere in the evening. I'm so sick of it. I refuse to marry a workaholic. That's it!"

One thing is for sure; Jean recognized one when she saw one. None of the "Well, I'll marry him, I can change him" bit. In refusing to marry Jack she may well have saved a divorce and a broken home later on.

Joe, a highly successful industrial engineer, was referred to a therapist. From all apparent signs he would appear to be a model of success and hard work. At thirty-four, he was the youngest top-management executive in his firm.

His fourteen-hour days had staggering agendas of meetings, conferences, and deadlines. He indicated to friends that he was a true workaholic. "I want more and more work. I chain-smoke cigarettes. I am arrogant. Like most compulsive workers, I have had this fantasy of omnipotence, that if I could just get over the next hurdle, everything would be all right."

Well, everything wasn't all right. One day Joe began to

9

feel dizzy at his desk and he felt a pain in his chest. It was like a band squeezing tighter and tighter. He suffered a heart attack, an all too frequent resuit of workaholism. His fantasy of omnipotence soon began to vanish as he became acutely aware of human limitations.

Joe was fortunate. He took his condition seriously and began to face up to his compulsion for work. He began to see that he had become emotionally dependent upon work; it had become an addiction to him.

Look around you, all around you—overworked individuals everywhere: government workers, executives, doctors, lawyers, preachers, school teachers, merchants. This may be your neighbor, or even your spouse. How about you? This book was written for every person who is caught in the numbers game. We live in an age of numbers: driver's license number, Social Security number, telephone numbers, and so forth. The workaholic has his own set of numbers: the long hours he works each day.

People caught in the work trap are often those who classically fit the saying, "He's working himself to death."

For many, it's a comfortable cop-out instead of facing life's greatest responsibilities. If you want to wreck your marriage, drive your kids away from you, and destroy most of your relationships—try overwork.

Here's the way you do it. It's simple and easy. Start staying late at work. Never say no. Take on more than you can possibly do in a work shift or in regular hours. And, by all means, bring your briefcase home piled high with work. Then, be sure to take on a part-time job a couple of nights a week or on the weekend. Or, load yourself with committee work. Accept every opportunity to serve!

The goal of this book is not primarily to impart knowledge. It has not been written simply to help you become a successful worker, but rather to help you to become a more fulfilled and successful human being.

This book makes no grand claims for remaking the world or any part of it. If you sense that you may have a problem because you may be in a work trap, it has been written to assist you with authentic relationships, individual responsibility, and in regaining the pleasure you once derived from work, as well as in helping you reassess what real living is all about.

You will note that this book is divided into three sections—I. The Conditions Regarding the Work Trap; II. The Causes Regulating the Work Trap; and III. The Cures Releasing the Work Trap—to help you in reaching these goals. Take heart—there is hope!

The authors want you to come to know yourself better—who you are and how you may become the better person you really want to be.

Not only is this book for those who are or may possibly become work addicts, it is for anyone who may need a bit more understanding about such a person who has chosen this pattern as a way of life. If you work with someone who makes you feel uncomfortable, such as the person who never looks at a clock and makes you feel guilty by his little glances or jibes when you are ready to leave the job at five o'clock, this book is for you as well. Somehow, you may perhaps feel he's after your job; he appears to be so dedicated. Within these pages you may receive a hint or two on how to deal with that situation, and many others.

Spouses and children stand in special need when they live with an individual who seems to need excessive work to survive. This individual needs much compassion. The authors hope you will gain the needed insight and emotional know-how to better cope with problems which may be threatening your well-being as a result of fractured relationships.

There is hope, but this nation has a serious problem on its hands.

If you're a workaholic, perhaps you're proud of your record, your perfectionistic standards, because you see them as strengths. "What's wrong with all this work? After all, it keeps me out of trouble and it provides me a way to bring home the bacon," you say.

Here's what's wrong: your addictive work behavior, instead of being a strength, serves as a real trap. It's a trap because you may not be doing at all what you really want to do. You work excessively because you really believe it is a necessity. The result of this conflict is strain and stress which may be eating at you like termites in a house.

Because of the changes and demands upon today's workers, particularly executives and professionals, anxiety and stress have become major problems for modern man in our highly industrialized nations. Over the past two decades, there have been innumerable changes which have accentuated the problem. Economics, politics, morality, ethical issues, and increasing crime all contribute to the current state of tension.

Millions of tranquilizers, endless articles and books speak of the uptight age of which we are a part. Few have been able to escape the anxiety of our times.

As much as we would like to avoid it, this anxiety is

here to stay. It won't go away. It influences the behavior of us all. Nothing is going to change this fact. So we had better not ignore it. We need to face it, rather than hiding our heads in the sand, pretending it doesn't exist or that it will somehow disappear.

Workaholism is a part of the growing problem because it is used hopefully as an escape from this kind of stress. This type of behavior is fast becoming a major American problem. In fact, it may be a disease endemic in all highly industrialized nations on earth.

We believe the need for this book is very great because there is no escaping the truth that the person who spends an overabundance of time at work creates tensions with far-reaching effects upon his personal life.

Part I

The Conditions Regarding the Work Trap

1

What Do You Mean—Workaholic?

Those who find time only for their jobs may often face severe consequences.

THE influence of our century affects not only national but individual tempos of living. The present world, with its numerous labor-saving devices, is quite different from the world of the thirteenth and fourteenth centuries, or even the nineteenth century. While it is true that these and other centuries preceding our own had their potentialities for speed and pressure living, man lacked the mechanical actualities to put these into effect.

Medieval men may have been driven by the increased tempo of their visions or conflicts, but they had considerable time to think and wait before they could learn of the effects. Today the telephone, the auto, and innumerable other devices have reduced this time to a minimum, while increasing individual and community activities to a maximum.

Man can now travel faster, exchange more ideas with more people, give out and receive orders for more work than ever before. The machines of the twentieth century pinnacled to new speed records with the jet and rocket planes, atomic energy, computers, and space travel.

Many of these external factors have combined to increase the tempo of living, but they have accomplished more than this. Through mass production, there has gradually emerged a tendency toward non-individualization of work. The slow and careful labor of the craftsmen of other days has been replaced by the assembly lines of the modern factory.

Where formerly man could see his own work from beginning to completion, he now sees but a small fragment of the whole. It is, therefore, not difficult to understand why tension is so much a twentieth-century product. With all our advances, in science especially, we may well ask ourselves whether the present-day speed of living, destructiveness, and non-individualization of work are conducive to health and to the best interests of man.

New Era for Man

The complexities of our highly industrialized modern world place many more and different demands upon the individual, especially in the workaday world. The twentieth century finds the Western world especially geared up for even more speed and greater accumulation of wealth. The industrial revolution has simply intensified the process of shortening the time between the desire for good and the capturing of it through hard work. More and more people become subject to the powerful demands of greed. They become consumed with efforts to *get.* In the process, they often hurl themselves upon the scrap heap of broken lives and relationships because they become things oriented rather than people centered.

The age of speed and acceleration also intensifies the problem. In the horse-and-buggy days (and we're not suggesting that we go back to those "good ol' days"), our grandfathers had time to talk leisurely to neighbors while their horses enjoyed a clump or two of grass along the road. But enveloped in the modern automobile, we seldom even get to see our neighbor as we whiz by him so much faster than at a racehorse clip.

If our great-grandparents missed the pony express, they'd be content to wait a week for the next one. Today, we get all bent out of shape if we miss our turn in the revolving door or the elevator.

The effects of the demands and stresses can be observed in

every aspect of modern life. The need to provide for one's survival demands that a person keep abreast with the inflationary spiral. One person was overheard saying to another, "When we were kids, ten cents was big money. How dimes have changed!" Keeping abreast economically is, in itself, a monumental task for today's worker.

In addition to change, advanced scientific technology and electronic wizardry, de-personalization, the demands of greed and economic survival, which all affect working conditions today, there is another extremely important and influential factor. In our modern world we live in an existential vacuum. Life for many is meaningless and purposeless. When men experience void and emptiness, they will try by any and all means to fill the vacuum or try to escape from that which is so meaningless. Addictive behavior is one solution that men may seek. Improper work attitudes and behavior is one form often chosen. Knowledge of occupational maladjustment is, therefore, important for a proper understanding of this kind of addictive behavior.

Numerous studies in the past fifteen years support the view that excessive work behavior is one of America's growing, serious problems which must be faced.

In an important study in Europe by Bransislav Cukic,[1] correlations were drawn showing that overload in work roles creates definite psychological problems. These problems diminish organizational efficiency and are a permanent source of stress, the study revealed.

S. M. Sales [2] submitted a research project to the University of Michigan in 1969, in which he studied responses to variations in work loads. He showed that men who have excessive work loads are subject to lower self-esteem, lower public esteem, higher cardiac rates, and more errors. He found that these effects disappeared sharply when the work overload was removed.

Wayne Oates, in his perceptive book *Confessions of a Workaholic*, [3] states that our land is full of workaholics and he sees the problem as a serious one. William H. Whyte, Jr., in his famous book, *The Organization Man*, [4] points out that an indi-

vidual who is so involved in his work that he cannot distinguish between work and the rest of life, is in trouble when it
comes to relationships.

Karl Menninger describes the addicted worker as one who
is void of love. Martin Haskell sees such individuals as rigid,
too controlled, without the ability to be spontaneous or free-
flowing in expressing emotions that tend toward closeness in
relationships.[5]

In a recently published article,[6] Charles White, M.D., Director of Gerontology at the University of Texas Health
Center, makes an astounding statement. He estimates that as
many as 50 percent of all white-collar workers in America are
workaholics. He calls them people who literally don't know
what to do with themselves if they are not working. He believes this problem is alarmingly on the increase.

Disease or Addiction, Which?

Well, just what is a *workaholic?* This term is in vogue right
now. Ten or fifteen years ago, it was not an English vocabulary
word. Now, you see it in more and more business journals and
articles written for popular magazines. We would have to say,
first of all, that it is a form of addiction. The *Psychiatric Dictionary* says:

> Addiction is considered to be a state of periodic or
> chronic intoxication, detrimental to the user and to soci-
> ety, produced by the repeated consumption . . . the user
> has lost the power of self-control.[7]

Webster's Third New International Dictionary defines an
addict as one who is completely possessed by a habit. The
addiction would then be a strong dependence, either
physiological or emotional, upon something external. It would
be a condition whereby the person needs to be given over to
the constant practice of intake in order to sustain the dependency upon it. There is a compulsive, overpowering quality
behind it. The longer the substance is used, the more the
process of conditioning or immunity deepens, creating a tendency to use the substance in ever-increasing amounts.

There is a difference between an addict and a user when it comes to alcohol or drugs. An alcoholic is one whose drinking interferes with a major department of his life on a continuing basis. It is a chronic, disabling, progressive malady which impairs the ability of the person to function in an acceptable manner in his environment. The addict has an overpowering desire to increase the dosage, a strong desire to continue his behavior, has a psychological and physiological dependency on the foreign substance, and there are detrimental effects to both society and the individual.

The user, on the other hand, may have a desire but there is no compulsion. There is little tendency to increase the dosage; there are few dependency needs, and any detrimental effects will only be to the individual himself.

These distinctions may be made with workers as well. As stated, many people love their work and work long hours. But there is no compulsion driving them to work and no dependency upon it. There are few detrimental effects.

Addictive behavior is a whole field of study today for the trained clinician. When we hear the word *addiction,* we usually only think of drugs, alcohol, or tobacco. Addiction is an adaptive technique, a way of coping with the anxieties and stresses of life. Workaholics in general learn that work relieves psychic pain and with increasing frequency use it as the solution to frustrations, anxieties, and depression. And, like other addictions, it works—at least for a time.

Origin of the Term *Workaholic*

Wayne Oates says the term *workaholic* is a neologism, an invented or semihumorous word for the addiction to work.[8]

We seldom think about it, but possibly one of the most unique and destructive of all addictions is the compulsion to work. We are beginning now to get a more serious understanding of the condition of *workaholism* where it exists. What adds to the seriousness of the problem is that it often goes untreated because it is the only addiction that makes one look like a saint rather than a sinner.

Workaholics are the people who always have more to do than they can ever complete. Their desks are rarely, if ever, cleared. They may appear to have a strong drive to achieve or to gain superiority. They appear to be so dedicated. Usually their inner strivings lie buried much deeper.

On one workaholic's office wall hung a plaque with this reminder: "Do a little more each day than everyone expects, and soon everyone will expect more."

In the book, *The Making of a Christian Leader*, this subject is addressed briefly:

> A person can become a "work-a-holic" by overcommitting himself financially, by making unrealistic plans, or simply by failing to recognize a personality defect. Often he may use work as an escape mechanism. Thus he has to drive himself to the exclusion of what should be his priorities.
>
> It is most unfortunate that we deplore drug and alcohol addicts but somehow promote and admire the work addict. We give him status and accept his estimate of himself. And all the while his family may be getting so little of his time and energy that they hardly know him.
>
> Overwork is not the disease itself. It is the symptom of a deeper problem—of tension, of inadequacy, of a need to achieve—that may have neurotic implications. Unfortunately for the work-a-holic, he has no home; his house is only a branch office. He won't take a vacation, can't relax, dislikes weekends, can't wait for Monday, and continues to make his own load heavier by bringing more work on to himself. Such a person also is usually defending against having to get close to people.[9]

On the Way Up or Down?

Gerald was a tall, handsome man in his late thirties. As an enterprising young executive with a large California electronics firm, he was definitely on the way up. One day he made an appointment with a psychotherapist. When asked the reason, he said that his wife had issued him an ultimatum.

"It's counseling or I'm leaving."

Subsequent counseling revealed that he was not merely an impatient man. He was a very harried one with a disproportionate amount of emotional energy consumed in struggling against the demands of time. Early in his private therapy, it was very evident that he could not relax. He moved about frequently and smoked one cigarette after another. He could seldom talk about himself, only his work. He dwelt incessantly upon it.

He admitted that he would love to play golf once a week, but stated that he just had no time for it. He had no hobbies. Rarely did he go to sporting events, museums, the zoo, or the symphony. He sometimes went to the movies but admitted to frequently falling asleep.

He wanted to be a good husband and father to his two children, but he admitted he didn't know how. He had noticed that his wife was getting involved in more activities outside their home. His children wriggled from his lap or grasp to run off to play. They knew his attention span with them was practically nil. "Daddy would rather read the *Wall Street Journal* or talk on the phone to some man about business."

When he talked with his wife in therapy sessions he seldom looked her in the eye. "It's the same at home," she stated. In conversation his mind was on other subjects. He had learned how to dutifully pretend to be involved. She knew better. "You're so isolated, I just can't reach you anymore." That was her last plea before demanding he go for help.

Gerald and Kathy just tolerated one another. There was no togetherness. They had struggled for years to communicate with each other. He said, "There's really nothing to talk about."

This story is typical of so many.

A recent survey of U.S. business executives, conducted by Paul R. Ray, whose firm surveyed 1,000 business leaders, 424 of whom responded, revealed the following astounding information.

The work week for executives surveyed averages over 50 hours—39 percent work 51–60 hours and 31 percent

reported working 46–50 hours. Only 6 percent work under
40 hours. work weeks averaging 60-plus hours are concen-
trated among those earning more than $60,000 annually.
Three out of four of those responding work nights, including business entertainment; more than half work at home
or on weekends . . . .

Only two out of three vacation regularly—47 percent
take two weeks and 46 percent take 3–4 weeks. Those
executives earning over $100,000 a year are much more
likely to skip vacations.[10]

One conclusion drawn from this survey is that the more one
earns the more he has to work. There is a price to pay for the
white-collar worker.

But there's your profile, Mr. Business Executive. Maybe you
found yourself listed in that group.

Speaking of executives who overwork, Alan N. Schoonmaker says:

Executives put in more hours at the office than the man
below, and they bring more work home at night. The
Executive Life survey found that one group (presidents,
vice-presidents, and high-potential middle managers)
worked between 57 and 60 hours a week. They spent 46 to
48 hours a week in the office during the day . . . and
worked at night three times a week. And this was during
normal times! When they had a trip, a convention, or an
emergency, they might put in 70 or 80 hours.[11]

The workaholic must come to grips with his form of idolatry.
Let's face it: the job becomes his god and the place of work is
the shrine. To the workaholic, the job has the highest priority
in life; therefore, he becomes overcommitted to it. Watch one,
there is some kind of a religious fervor or devotion about it all.

Wayne Oates has an interesting comment at this point:

Work, furthermore, can become the special addiction of
the religious man. The monks of Cluny could say that "to
work is to pray." This meant something quite different,

however, from saying that work itself is the god to whom we pray, the god whom we propitiate with our bodies for the sins of our spirits, the idol who enslaves us. Addiction to work is not far from the disorder of the monasteries known as *acedia*, earlier classified by Johannes Cassianus (*ca.* 5th century A.D.) as one of the seven deadly sins. *Acedia* was defined by Evagius Ponticus as the condition in a monk that made him fall asleep in his cell or else desert his religious work altogether. It stemmed from the fact that the religious man's work had gone beyond the point of increasing returns: he worked more and more and accomplished less and less, becoming all the while more and more bored with and anxious over his work.[12]

Of such things, workaholics are born. It becomes a habit of life later on. And, even when they are not working, they will often occupy their minds with work. They are either reading something related to it or they are thinking about it.

Dead Ends

The workaholic, whether innocently or by design, has placed himself in the noncaring, noninvolvement position. All caring has hazards, since one who is involved is vulnerable to being hurt and a painless outcome can never be guaranteed. But noninvolvement also exacts a price in terms of lost satisfactions, feelings of estrangement and alienation, and a lack of meaning in one's existence. The workaholic fits this description in a general sense because he is in a noninvolvement position with people close to him.

People may consider the workaholic to be a success and a dedicated person. One company president said of an executive who was a classical workaholic: "He makes one heck of a contribution to our company."

But in most cases, if such a person stays on the job for any great length of time, problems will begin. Absenteeism may set in because of great pressures in the home. He may be forced into having to deal with situations such as the work-and-success-oriented father who never spent time with his boy. Now he has to take the time to go to Juvenile Hall and stand in court alongside his son.

Sometimes the workaholic is a bad manager because he frequently doesn't know how to work with people. He usually does not delegate his work because of his illusions. "Nobody can do this work like me," he tells himself. He also doesn't delegate work because he does not trust others. Certainly excellence in work cannot be sustained if a worker believes he must do it all himself.

Do workaholics go very far? In a published magazine article, Dr. Frederic Flack, a New York psychiatrist who has treated many people with work problems, reports that because of their diligence they tend to keep getting promoted in corporations. However, he says, a lack of imagination keeps them from reaching the top rungs in business. They make great salesmen but very poor corporation presidents. Because of their lack of creativity, they rarely make any original contributions to the welfare of mankind and they usually end up in upper-middle management, dispensing grief to everyone.

Dr. Flack goes on to note that continual work violates one of the basic rules for coming up with original solutions—to move into another area and let the problems simmer. He adds that one reason workaholics work such long hours is that they are not finding ways to think about something in a new and creative way. They get all hung up. They can't be creative because creativity looks like idleness to them.[13]

There is not only less creativity, but, in the long run, the workaholic will often contribute less to the growth of the firm or organization because his unbalanced attitude toward life will begin to catch up with him in counterproductive ways. One admitted workaholic reported not long ago, "I began to recognize that I spent twelve to fourteen hours of time at work getting paid for only six to eight hours of work." This inevitably leads to hostility. The firm as well as the individual stands to lose. If ever the law of diminishing returns were applicable, it is in this area.

There Is a Difference

One of the easiest things to do is to attach labels to people. Yes, upon our friends and neighbors as well as upon those we do not know. We need to recognize the fact that many people work long and hard. This does not necessarily mean that they should be classified as workaholics.

We have to be careful. We should not confuse the thousands of workaholics with those who love their work. One of the major differences seems to be that the work lover can stop when he wants to. He does not have an emotional need to consume himself with work. He can walk away from the office, shop, or store and leave it there.

It is easy to label a person a workaholic when he actually is not, for there are innumerable individuals who really do enjoy their work. History demonstrates this very clearly. People like Mark Twain, Thomas Edison, Henry Ford, Albert Schweitzer, and Leonardo da Vinci considered their work also their play.

The workaholic, however, doesn't stop working and he has no fun at it. As a matter of fact, few of them have any sense of humor.[14] "He's so consumed with work that he has crowded everything else out of his life, even the comics and the sports page," said one wife about her husband.

While most everyone may think of a workaholic as a great success, a little probing will prove that in many cases he is a failure as a father and husband.

We need to bear in mind that most people, at times, experience the symptoms of workaholism. Anyone who is truly active and busy will have a tendency to get locked in at given times. Good examples are tax consultants from January through April or sales clerks during the Christmas rush. When the crunch lets up they may go into a mild depression and not know what to do with themselves. However, they will usually pull out of it in short order. They are not chronic addicts, however, because their pain will begin to ebb, their spirits perk up, and they will soon be back to normal.

A great many Americans today work hard and play hard. But

some just work, either from the unquenchable love of it or from a deep-seated compulsion beyond their control.

Let's face it, work lovers, for whatever reason, provide society with many leaders in the community—business, science, religion, politics, education, arts, and sports. Many, however, pay a dear price. Their addiction can lead to dead-end careers, to marriage break-ups, to poor health, and even to death. They are so emotionally dependent upon work that without it they begin to fall apart.

The pure, unadulterated workaholic may be rare, but there is a little of him in almost everyone. It is well to consider the warning signals before becoming drunk with the addiction.

Remember, you can OD on too much work.

2

What Good Is Work Anyway?

Any man who has a job has a chance.

PROBABLY the complaint we Americans make most often is in regard to the weather. Running a close second are our comments concerning work. "Oh, if only I didn't have to go to work today. What a drag!" "I'd quit work forever if it wasn't for my wife and family." "Work . . . what a necessary evil." How often we have heard or used these types of comments.

Almost as much has been written about work as about love. Many famous people have commented on it. Bismarck once said, "To youth I have but three words of counsel—work, work, work" (*Sayings of Bismarck*). Jerome K. Jerome said, "I like work; it fascinates me. I can sit and look at it for hours" (*Three Men in a Boat*, chapter 15). "Any man who has a job has a chance," said Elbert Hubbard (*Epigrams*).

Others take a pessimistic view. That old cynic, Mark Twain, once said, "Let us be grateful to Adam, our benefactor. He cut us out of the 'blessing' of idleness and won for us the 'curse' of labor" (*Pudd'nhead Wilson's Calendar*).

What is work, anyway? It is not easy to define. You hear many definitions ranging from "that activity which renders payment for service rendered, such as earning money, making a living," to "that activity which occupies one's time during most of his waking hours." It could also be "the activity for which one utilizes his skills in some employment situation."

29

We are using the term *work* in a sense broad enough to include the white-collar person, the blue-collar worker, the top manager, homemakers, and even volunteers. Obviously, there are many variations and types of work done, depending on educational and cultural factors. Despite the differences, there are enough similarities to provide a basic meaning which is common to all.

Coleman and Hammen define work as "an activity that produces something of value for other people." [1]

But, as Lloyd Lofquist points out, if work is truly the focal point for the development of one's way of life and a means to adjust to it, then these definitions are inadequate. [2] He states that from the earliest of time, work was seen as a curse or form of punishment and it became a means of atoning for sin.

We do know that the ancient Greeks used the word *ponos* for work, which connoted drudgery. They associated it with sorrow and a burdensome experience. The ancient Hebrews saw it as a heavy yoke but believed it had value. Rabbis, for example, were expected to have a trade of some kind.

Later, Christianity added a positive value. Work was seen as a means of charity which lifted the concept to mean that through it the Kingdom of God would be fashioned on earth.

> With the passing of the centuries, a distinction developed between work that was intellectual, spiritual, contemplative, and work that was manual, physical, exertive. The medieval universities, for instance, distinguished between the liberal arts and the servile arts (Pieper, 1952). The servile arts were undertaken for the satisfaction of basic human needs. The liberal arts could not be put at the disposal of such utilitarian, albeit necessary, ends. Performance of a liberal art could not, rightly speaking, be paid for. The honorarium was nothing more than a contribution given towards the liberal artist's living expenses. On the other hand, a wage meant payment earned for a servile art, that is, for a particular piece of work, and with no necessary reference to the cost-of-living needs of the worker.[3]

Through the Middle Ages and with the addition of the philosophy of the Protestant reformers, work had three basic meanings:

(1) work was a hard necessity, painful and burdensome; (2) work was instrumental, a means toward ends, especially religious ends; and (3) work was the creative act of man, therefore intrinsically good.[4]

These three views appear to be the basic ideal still prevalent today although they are increasingly being undermined.

Well, whether we like it or not, work is a vital part of our lives. If you don't think so, consider this. Even though the study of the psychological aspects of the loss of work owing to retirement has not been thoroughly investigated, have you noticed what so often happens to individuals when they retire?

Many of them die shortly thereafter. Of many of those who live, their wives complain because "the ol' man" just doesn't know what to do with himself. Some wives have been distraught, not knowing how to handle having him around all day.

There is a drastic change of pace. One moment the man has authority, the next he is without any. The workaholic will particularly suffer in this readjustment setting. One of his penalties is that when the trauma of retirement faces him, he finds it extremely difficult to change because he doesn't have adequate emotional equipment to make the necessary adjustments. It is generally because he lacks the spontaneity and flexibility to make them.

Perhaps the primary reason for the adjustment difficulties of people entering the retirement years is the fact that work is such an important phase of life. In fact, it is an extension of oneself. You may have noticed that when people meet for the first time, so very often the first question asked is, "What do you do?" "I'm a lawyer. What do *you* do?" "I'm an accountant."

When a man loses his job, have you observed how he is

treated? It would seem it's almost like having leprosy! He's avoided like a plague. Suddenly, it seems his friends drop him. He and his wife don't get invited out nearly as frequently as formerly. Often his golf buddies drop him. He becomes a misfit. That's why if ever a man is out of work, he really needs his friends.

There's no escaping it: work is an institution. In fact, it is most basic because it actually helps to maintain survival. Much has been written about the work ethic over the centuries from religious, philosophical, moral, political, and psychological backgrounds. In his work, a person probably expends more energy over a lifetime than in any other kind of activity, and with the increase of life expectancy in our society, we may easily expect a person to average fifty years of his life working.

For most people, work is something that must be done. Thus, to many, it has a negative ring to it. However, psychologists have concluded that work has a crucial psychological bearing on life, for work provides important personal and social functions and outlets for the one working. These would, of course, include the need for achievement, personal worth, and self-identity.

Increasingly, people in our society are coming to realize once again the value of work in their quest for meaningfulness. In the 1960s, there was a mass movement away from the idea of the dignity of work. There was flight away from the realities of personal responsibility. The hippie mentality played down the important aspects of work. Now we are coming full circle. The self-defining and potentially self-fulfilling aspects of work should be considered to be significant insights for today's expanding world, for money and wages are seen not merely as ends in themselves.

Work Develops Personality

Let us consider the meaning of work in terms of the individual. The value judgment inherent in the message of this book is that work ought to be and can be a deeply fulfilling and meaningful part of man's existence.

There are many positive effects of work upon people. The first is that through work a person is able to expend energy in a wholesome and acceptable way. The psychologist calls this sublimation. Therefore, work constitutes an important factor providing for equilibrium and development of the personality. Through it, man comes in better contact with reality and the meaning of his own existence. This was acutely felt by Sigmund Freud in one of his last books, in which he explained the role played by work.

> Stressing the importance of work has a greater effect than any other technique of living in binding the individual more closely to reality; in his work he is at least securely attached to a part of reality, the human community. Work is no less valuable for the opportunity which it, and the human relations connected with it, provide for a very considerable discharge of fundamental libidinal impulses, narcissistic, aggressive and even erotic, than because it is indispensable for subsistence and justifies existence in society. The daily work of earning a livelihood affords especial satisfaction. It enables use to be made of existing inclinations, of instinctual impulses, hitherto repressed, or more intense than usual for constitutional reasons.[5]

Freud is right because he saw work as a balancing factor in a person's life, fitting him into the sociological structure of the human family, and enhancing his ability to make some contribution to that very society. Work, for better or for worse, helps a person change his environment and, yes, even himself. Georges Friedmann says:

> It is work that raises man, as soon as he produces his own means of subsistence, above biological time and gives character to human history, of whose movements it is at once the explanation and the underlying cause . . . . It is not surprising that an activity which is essential as a determinant of species as well as in the

history of human societies should be just as essential a determinant for the individual microcosm, enabling him to understand his successes and his failures, his own individual history.[6]

Certainly one way to ascertain the importance of work in a person's life is to observe how men act when they are deprived of it. Strong feelings of insecurity usually occur right after the initial shock, which creates intense anxiety in most people. If an individual finds it increasingly difficult to work, depression of varying degrees may result. A feeling of inadequacy may be a tag-along, too, because self-esteem is jarred. Indeed, the loss of the settled framework of a job is enormous. One can hardly imagine that his peace of mind and control over one's family are so dependent upon a steady job.

Freud is right. Work does connect a person with his community.

It may be a very long time before we can fully comprehend all the underlying unconscious motives involved in the various aspects of human labor. But one thing appears to be true. The energy of aggressive needs in work can be a good force. A destructive impulse drive can be modified through the constructive activity of work.

This can be illustrated in many ways. The doctor who fights malaria, the teacher who fights prejudice, the minister who fights sin, all use a refined type of aggression. This energy is directed towards destructive forces or enemies of mankind.

Such sublimated energy is good. In such activities the worker, by using his aggressive drives to help others, also helps himself. Thus we see first that work serves as a means of expressing the life force, helping one to balance out his life and to drain off energy in acceptable ways. As an extension of oneself, it helps to upgrade a person's self-esteem because it gives him a sense of worth and dignity, especially if he experiences some achievement.

Good Therapy

"Why do people work?" is an oft-asked question. People do need to support themselves, but that is not always the dominant inspiration. Many may work because they prefer to be doing something rather than nothing, and because they may fear the social censure which is directed against idlers and loafers. But the value of work lies deeper than this. Otherwise, why would people work diligently without being paid for their services? All about us there is a great deal of volunteer work. And what about the best example of all, the faithful, uncomplaining housewife who may spend as much time, and often more, working in her home than her husband does at the office or shop!

When there is stress, work can oftentimes be very therapeutic, particularly if taken in reasonable doses. A man can go through a painful divorce or experience much grief over the loss of a loved one. He can come back to work and immediately get absorbed in his activity. The work then serves a useful purpose. It can be a wonderful form of therapy. After a period of time, mental—and physical—health may be restored.

Of course a person should not be sent out on a job until emotionally and physically ready. Recovery usually accelerates when a person is able to hold down a responsible job. It restores to him a sense of dignity and worth.

Examples abound which reveal the therapeutic value of finding fulfillment in a job situation.

Greater Satisfaction

People who are contented with their working conditions are bound to be much more fulfilled. Where there are dissatisfactions over job conditions, the pay, the fellow workers, or the nature of the work, there may be many psychological consequences that will yield repercussions later on. For example, people who feel like they count for little on the job may develop psychosomatic ills. They may be afraid to react, to allow themselves to feel or be understood. Anxiety, worry, hypertension, and loss of self-esteem are often direct results.

Studies reveal that greater mental health problems exist in jobs that are dull, unchallenging, repetitive, and allow for little advancement. A deadening effect is created where people find their jobs exerting heavy pressure and responsibility and where there are not the accompanying status, security, and salary rewards.

But where satisfaction exists in a job the person usually experiences greater meaning in his life. By self-fulfillment we mean that a person will be restless and discontented unless he is really doing what he is fitted for or capable of performing.

In a study by George Andrew Sargeant, it was found that individuals who perceive a relatively clear purpose and meaning in their lives are more work motivated. The study revealed that there were significant differences between individuals with high and low "Purpose in Life" scores in terms of their attitudes toward work (that is, the meaning of work).[7] There is, then, a relationship between the perception of meaning in life and the perceived meaning of work and other major life concepts.

When discussing the subject of need satisfaction, we must include Abraham Maslow's views. He basically sought to determine the basic drives of the human personality and how they are satisfied. His thoughts, therefore, have a bearing on the work situation and its meaning for life.

His theory about needs has application in all areas of life even though it has been challenged. Maslow assumes that all individuals have a basic set of needs which they strive to fulfill. His theory looks like this:

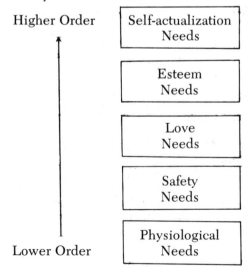

Maslow states that all individuals will always strive to satisfy basic needs before higher-order needs and they will move up the hierarchy in a systematic manner, satisfying the lower needs before moving upward.

This theory has been a popular one in management circles because Maslow's theory is related to industrial behavior, since individuals will strive to fulfill all these needs in a work setting.

A person's philosophy about work will affect his outlook and the fulfillment needs which he deems necessary for meaningful living. This theory tells us that it is essential to know what needs the individual is trying to satisfy, since this will provide clues about an employee's motivation toward satisfaction. This implies, then, that a person will instigate, direct, and sustain activity at work to satisfy certain needs. Thus, it is helpful for a person to know which of his needs have the highest priority.

Reflecting on Maslow's views, it should be noted that human satisfaction is brief and is never complete. It is difficult to accurately measure the degree of satisfaction or dissatisfaction of a worker with his job because there are no absolute values which can be used to measure job satisfaction.

Debate exists today among management theoreticians and industrial psychologists concerning the problem of whether human satisfaction can be achieved on the job or outside the job—that is, is human motivation an integral part of the mental makeup of man or can outside factors motivate man toward greater effort?

Maslow regards the satisfaction of human needs as the key motivator in human economic activity. As noted, once a need is satisfied, it ceases to serve as a motivator. This role is then taken over by the successive need in the hierarchy.

As a result of this chain reaction, human satisfaction is always of a short duration. Thus, man cannot reach total satisfaction except, perhaps, for a short duration.

But Maslow overlooks the fact that the unsatisfied craving of man may be a product of our civilization. Culture will be important in pronouncing the value placed on work. Also, it is true that aspirations of men may vary greatly from one group to another or from one individual to another. Drives within people will be determined by social or cultural backgrounds.

Also, it must be remembered that men are driven by both rational and irrational motives. Maslow overemphasizes the importance of the rational. People may not have the desire to satisfy needs at the higher level of the hierarchy. They may also be prevented from moving upward because their perception of the degrees of satisfaction may vary.

That is why it is important for management, for example, to try to determine whether at a given point physical or social needs are the most significant when it comes to motivating a person on the job. In other words, at which stage is it more important to pat a person on the back or provide extra dollars in wages?

There does often seem to be a tendency within management to overemphasize the on-the-job problems without probing for underlying problems which decrease job satisfaction.

There is also the question of whether it is possible to make all jobs equally interesting to all people, and, if so, how to match up each worker with a suitable job. What is regarded by one person as desirable may be completely undesirable for another.

Studies reveal another insight. The common assumption is that a happy worker is a good producer. This is not always true. High morale is a positive factor in human motivation, but it does not necessarily follow that it will in every case increase productivity. There is no substitute for proper managerial leadership and planned coordination among the workers.

But one thing does appear certain. A person who achieves higher satisfaction on the job has a higher degree of capability to cope with outside problems and interests.

It is unfortunate that so many people see their work as meaningless. They will so often try to relieve the emptiness by joking, idling, or seeking to outwit management.

When it's all said, it can hardly be assumed that for the most part people do not value their work. Though many today "goof off" or refuse to work, other responsible people, in fact, may consider their work as an end in itself. Especially is this true for the professional who sees work as a focal center for his self-identification. His work may become a central life interest, giving his living a great deal of meaning and purpose.

Most business and professional people view their work in terms of a career rather than a job. They depend on their work not only to structure their day but to provide some sense of adequacy which gives them a sense that they are living up to their potential as well as their education.

In contradistinction, the unemployed prove the significance and meaning of work when they talk about a sense of lostness without work. Others find such idleness as almost unbearable, sometimes worse than being without food and clothing. Often a sense of hopelessness prevails with them.

Work done for its own sake, enjoyed for its own intrinsic value, is within the reach of anyone who wants it by virtue of the freedom man has to choose his lot in life. Through it a person develops self-worth, resolution of conflicts, and greater satisfaction.

3

What Does the Bible Say?

*Let him that stole steal no more: but
rather let him labour, working with
his hands the thing which is
good . . . .*

Ephesians 4:28

A GRADUATE engineering student was placed in a good job.
After five years he surprised one of his companions by stating,
"I would quit tomorrow if I had a chance. If only I had the
money to retire. The only reason I work is to give me something to do and to keep my family in food and clothes."

What does the church have to say to this young man who is
obviously unfulfilled and bored with his job? Does theology
have anything to offer? Admittedly, millions of Americans are
churchgoers. Religious fervor of every type is on the increase.
Christian literature sells more rapidly than ever before. The
Christian market has top priority, not only with Christian publishing houses but with secular publishers as well.

Yet it seems that fewer people "live close to God" in a truly
meaningful way. Fewer still seem able to make the applica-
tions of divine truth to their personal lives. Perhaps it is due to
the forces of secularization, scientific rationalism, and the
socialistic schemes found today.

The workaday world today is a very different matter than
was the case centuries ago. Distinctions that once existed between the Christian and non-Christian worker are becoming
blurred. The church may be partly to blame for this. Its emphasis often appears to be mainly upon subjective experience

and personal piety. Of course this is important. But where is the emphasis upon personal application in the great bastions of our society as well as in one's own private affairs, in his own small environment?

The man in the pew is told to go out and take the world for God. But how?

In a study by Raymond Baumhart,[1] a number of business managers were asked, "How much guidance did your church and clergymen provide for the ethical problems you and your business acquaintances faced in the last five years?" Here are the tabulated questionnaire results: About the right amount—16 percent; some, but not enough—25 percent; none—35 percent; can't say—23 percent; too much—1 percent. Baumhart concluded that about four out of every five businessmen were dissatisfied with what organized religion had to offer or say regarding the problems facing businessmen.

This is a sad tale. Few ministers have had much economic training or study. They are sorely ignorant concerning business matters. This is not always by choice, but sometimes by design. Theological leaders see very little purpose in such an educational pursuit for clergy.

One of Baumhart's respondents, a young New York stockbroker, stated, "The average clergyman has such a scant understanding of the U.S. economy that his intervention in this area would be a mistake." A Louisiana insurance broker said, "I don't believe the clergy should be permitted to preach to businessmen." And the vice-president of a large cement plant in the East recently stated, "In the natural cycle of life—birth, marriage and death—the church is doing a fine job, but it is nonexistent when decisions are being made in a man's line of work."

Baumhart did conclude that most business people do welcome the assistance of theologians who are educated in business concerns.

When they do speak out responsibly, far too few Christians make the transition of practical Christianity from the Sunday school classroom or sanctuary to their workaday world. There is a need for theologians and social scientists to work together to help in the application process. Theology can make a significant contribution to the workaday world, as it has in the past two decades in the areas of race relations and civil rights.

By theology is meant an understanding of God and His work through history. It is not faith. Faith is subjective; theology is objective. It needs to be incorporated by faith to effect change. Theology then is an understanding of faith, especially regarding God's revelation of Himself and of His great and indescribable love for man.

There is a Christian way of life that must be applied. There are Christian principles that can help us in our daily economic actions. Faith and reason blended together can be of great incentive to men to labor with proper attitudes. It is self-evident that in all our labors we should choose the most efficient, the most economic methods. All Christians should seek to provide for the legitimate wants and needs of their fellowmen as they provide for their own through work. This requires what economists call "the division of labor." All Christians should exchange the fruits of their specialized, and therefore more proficient, labors for the profit of their neighbors as well as themselves. Christians should refrain from envy, force, or fraud.

But where do such ideals originate? The greatest textbook for life is the Bible—both the Old and New Testaments. And, issuing from the Holy Scriptures is our Judeo-Christian heritage.

The Bible has a great deal to say about work. Ruth gleaned in the fields when romance caught up with her. Gideon was working on the threshing floor when the angel of the Lord spoke to him about another kind of work. How about Moses the sheepherder? Just remember the personalities we meet in the Bible. It is a book written by workers, written about workers, written to workers. It is a book that is vitally relevant for today's world. Every aspect of life comes under its scrutiny. This includes our work philosophy, attitudes, and habits.

Here is a partial list of familiar Bible personalities who were cited in their work:

Noah,		Naaman	soldier
Boaz	farmers	Jonathan	warrior
Moses	shepherd	Ezra	reformer
Joseph,		Isaiah	historiographer
Daniel	prime ministers	Amos	herdsman
Gideon,		Matthew	tax collector
Samson,		Peter,	
Samuel	judges	James,	
Eli	priest	John	fishermen
David	musician,	Luke	physician
	king	Paul	writer,
Solomon	lyric poet		missionary
Hiram	artisan	Lydia	saleswoman
Naboth	grape grower	Titus	social worker
Elijah,			
Jonah	prophets		

Can you add to this list? There are many more persons. It is interesting to note how often God spoke to men when they were faithfully at work, not in a state of idleness. It is as though God were blessing their labor.

For example, when did God call Moses? When he was tending his flocks. What were the shepherds doing in the Christmas story when they were told by an angel of the birth of the Saviour? "Keeping watch over their flocks by night." When did Jesus call Peter? When he looked up from his fishing nets. Matthew was called while counting money as a tax collector.

When Jesus taught the multitudes He often alluded to work situations. His illustrations often centered around vinedressers, farmers, builders, and magistrates. He told of managers and farmhands. And, He spoke of them in a favorable manner.

Work Instituted by God

The first significant statement about work in the Bible is its relationship to man's fallen condition: "In the sweat of thy face shalt thou eat bread, till thou return unto the ground . . ." (Genesis 3:19). First, we must bear in mind that work was ordained by God. Because man was told after our

first father sinned that he would have to work by the sweat of
his brow does not mean that labor is a penalty for sin. The
Bible never considers work a curse.

Adam had the job of caring for the Garden of Eden before he
ate of the forbidden fruit. Work was thus instituted and
blessed by God. People in the world may adopt theft as a way
of life, but the biblically inspired individual knows that it is
not a shame to be caught working.

God Himself was a worker. Numerous times in the Scriptures this point is made.

> Thus the heavens and the earth were finished, and all
> the host of them. And on the seventh day God ended his
> work which he had made; and he rested on the seventh
> day from all his work which he had made. And God
> blessed the seventh day, and sanctified it: because that in
> it he had rested from all his work which God created and
> made.
>
> Genesis 2:1-3

The emphasis is upon ceasing rather than upon resting. The
associated word in English is the word *pause,* the word *rest*
being used in something of the same sense as it is today in the
technical language of music.

God Commands Work

The Bible frequently records the fact that God has commanded work to specific people. Hence, it must be deduced
that work has a profitable purpose.

In the Ten Commandments God says, "Six days shalt thou
labour, and do all thy work" (Exodus 20:9).

The Lord spoke to Moses on one occasion, citing Bezaleel to
be a craftsman to help build the tabernacle during Israel's
wilderness wanderings after they left Egypt.

> And I have filled him with the spirit of God, in wisdom,
> and in understanding, and in knowledge, and in all man-
> ner of workmanship, to devise cunning works, to work in
> gold, and in silver, and in brass, And in cutting of stones,

to set them, and in carving of timber, to work in all manner of workmanship.   Exodus 31:3–5

When the Jews were defeated by Nebuchadnezzar in 586 B.C., thousands were carried off to Babylonia. During the seventy-year captivity, God inspired some of their leaders to go back to Jerusalem and rebuild the city walls and the sacred temple. Cyrus, the king of Babylon, gave his consent. One of the leaders given this tremendous assignment by God was Nehemiah. He indicated that the work was initiated by God:

And it came to pass, that when all our enemies heard thereof, and all the heathen that were about us saw these things, they were much cast down in their own eyes: for they perceived that this work was wrought of our God.
                                    Nehemiah 6:16

Haggai, one of the Jewish prophets living during this period of rehabilitation, speaks the Word of God:

Yet now be strong, O Zerubbabel, saith the Lord; and be strong, O Joshua . . . all ye people of the land, saith the Lord, and work: for I am with you . . . .
                                    Haggai 2:4

Work Is Honorable

Work in the Old Testament, whether related to the ancient walls or the Temple in Jerusalem or secular employment, was seen as honorable. The following passages disclose the blessedness and dignity of work.

And the Levite, (because he hath no part nor inheritance with thee,) and the [sojourner], and the fatherless, and the widow, which are within thy gates, shall come, and shall eat and be satisfied; that the Lord thy God may bless thee in all the work of thine hand which thou doest.
                                    Deuteronomy 14:29

When thou cuttest down thine harvest in thy field, and hast forgot a sheaf in the field, thou shalt not go again to fetch it: it shall be for the [sojourner], for the fatherless, and for the widow: that the Lord thy God may bless thee in all the work of thine hands.   Deuteronomy 24:19

The Lord shall open unto thee his good treasure, the
heaven to give the rain unto thy land in his season, and to
bless all the work of thine hand . . . .

Deuteronomy 28:12

We read in Job of God's blessing upon him: "Thou hast
blessed the work of his hands, and his substance is increased
in the land" (Job 1:10).

Solomon, in proclaiming the wisdom of God, states that God
has ordained time for work: "For there is a time there for every
purpose and for every work" (Ecclesiastes 3:17). Other passages that help us to see that work is honorable are 1 Chronicles 16:37 and 2 Chronicles 31:21; 34:9–12.

Praise and Reward for Work

Nehemiah praises the faithful people who worked to rebuild the ancient walls of Jerusalem around 500 B.C. "So built
we the wall: and all the wall was joined together unto the half
thereof: for the people had a mind to work" (Nehemiah 4:6).
One of the ancient historians in the nation of Israel wrote: "Be
ye strong, therefore, and let not your hands be weak: for your
work shall be rewarded" (2 Chronicles 15:7).

Work Is Good

The wisdom literature of the ancient Jews abounds with the
high place of work in one's life. For example, the housewife is
praised because of her faithful work (*see* Proverbs 31:13–31).

During the foundation of the monarchy of ancient Israel,
after the sojourn in Egypt, the nation was organized into a
great work force. We find these interesting words in the ancient record:

And these are the singers, [heads] of the fathers of the
Levites, who remaining in the chambers were free: for
they were employed in that work day and night.

1 Chronicles 9:33

The New Testament endorses this idea as well: ". . . do your own business, and to work with your own hands, as we commanded you" (1 Thessalonians 4:11).

Satisfaction in Work

Economics and work are more closely related to the Bible than many appreciate. Isaiah the prophet illustrates how the two are related. The demand for satisfaction in work lies back of his question: "Wherefore do you spend money for that which is not bread? and your labour for that which satisfieth not? . . ." (Isaiah 55:2).

Isaiah suggests that the demand for work satisfaction leads to many derived demands, such as for bread and labor which produces goods which may contribute to satisfaction. "Derived demand" is a familiar concept to economists.

Paul, in the New Testament, refers to work satisfaction when he says: "Let every man prove his own work, and then shall he have rejoicing in himself alone . . ." (Galatians 6:4).

Productive Work Effort

The Book of Proverbs deals with more economic themes than any other Old Testament book. One important principle which the writer sets forth is Proverbs 6:6: "Go to the ant, thou sluggard; consider her ways, and be wise." Many visionaries tell us that automated machinery has abolished the Victorian work ethic. No one will have to work or save anymore. We can all be grasshoppers. Those who are seeing the magic of an "economy of abundance" in their crystal balls should ponder Aesop's fable of the grasshopper and the ant, along with Proverbs. While they eulogize the ways of the grasshopper, we would do well to emulate the ways of the ant.

Another proverb supports the same basic concept. "Wealth gotten by vanity shall be diminished: but he that gathereth by labour shall increase" (Proverbs 13:11). This proverb seems to be saying that you cannot depend upon wealth gotten by any means other than productive effort or work and that such work will increase productivity.

Wealth may be made by speculation, which is not always bad. Speculation is sometimes of positive benefit to the economy, but the speculative gains of today are often the losses of tomorrow.

Wealth may be given to one. There is nothing wrong with gifts and they are not always squandered, but the old rule "easy come—easy go" has a way of attaching itself to wealth received as a gift.

Wealth may be stolen, but thieves rarely succeed in keeping their ill-gotten gains.

The Divine Calling to Work

Christianity lifts labor into a higher sphere where the problems which loom large to the secular mind become irrelevant. In Christianity, the grace of God redeems labor and changes it into joyous work. In fact, it makes work a divine calling. It gives man identity as one made in the image of God.

Not only is the Christian exhorted to work (Ephesians 4:28), but the Christian's occupation itself is selected by God. Thus, the Puritans produced tracts with such titles as "Husbandry Spiritualized," "The Religious Weaver," and "The Tradesman's Calling." This kind of faith enables any work because it brings to the believer the realization that he is cooperating with God in performing the most menial task. As John Calvin said:

> This, too, will afford admirable consolation, that in following your proper calling, no work will be so mean and sordid as not to have a splendour and value in the eye of God.

There is a familiar story which illustrates this view of labor. A traveller asked three men at work what they were doing. The first replied that he was earning his living; the second that he was laying bricks; but the third answered, with a glow in his eyes, "Sir, I am building a cathedral." The third man expressed the Christian view of work as a divine calling—a cooperating with God in accomplishing His purpose on earth.

After the death of Christ, the Christian church entered what we know as the Apostolic period. Those who had seen Christ and lived to write about it shed much light on the Christian concept of work. The Apostle Paul informed the church at Corinth that he was a good worker, defending his accountability as a good steward of his time and ministry (1 Corinthians 4:12). As a professional missionary, he still believed it important to labor with his hands. He made tents when he was not preaching.

There are those today who still hold that a servant of God should help to support himself by his own hands like Paul, who acquired both a knowledge of the Scriptures and worked at a trade. Luke alluded to Paul's occupation in Acts 18:2–3. Paul, on several occasions, spoke with pride about his honorable work.

Thus, by his personal example as well as in his exhortation, Paul set an example for the early Christian community when it came to honest work. In his epistle to the church at Ephesus he said:

> Let him that stole steal no more: but rather let him labour, working with his hands the thing which is good, that he may have to give to him that needeth.
>
> Ephesians 4:28

Paul teaches that work is a man's right. Work is a duty, but it is also a privilege.

The Ephesian passage supports the Ten Commandments. "Thou shalt not steal" and "Thou shalt not covet" place strong emphasis upon the individual's seeking other ways to support himself.

The New Testament never reversed the Old Testament dictum that God gives "power to get wealth" (Deuteronomy 8:18) although, to be sure, it does warn that the wealthy should show compassion in the use of their wealth. Paul urges Christians to work in order to "have" so that they may "give to those who are in need."

Again, Paul states, "For even when we were with you, this we commanded, that if any would not work, neither should he eat" (2 Thessalonians 3:10). (This passage might be a good one for parents to remember on occasion!)

The Apostle, in defining the model walk of the believer, wrote in his first letter to the church of Thessalonica,

> And that ye study to be quiet, and to do your own business, and to work with your own hands, as we commanded you; that ye may walk honestly toward them that are without, and that ye may have lack of nothing.
>
> 1 Thessalonians 4:11–12

Lydia was another early Christian convert noted for her work. She continued to dye her woolens after her conversion. In her example we see that work was an integral part of the whole scheme of life in biblical Judaism and New Testament Christianity.

This brief study from both the Old and New Testaments gives us an idea of the importance that work plays in our lives and what a proper attitude should be. Work was initiated by God, is honorable, blessed, and rewarded. There is an accountability to faithful work because it is good. It provides a basic satisfaction for living, and people may expect productive efforts from it.

Some Practical Applications

Sometimes Christians have the mistaken idea that unless they are in a full-time, church-related occupation they are not really serving God. In some circles the missionary is considered to be most in tune with God's will, followed in turn by the pastor, other full-time Christian workers, and then "those who have compromised with the world." The Bible gives no support to this thinking. There is never any suggestion that one form of work is better or more significant than another.

As we have seen, the Judeo-Christian concept of work is evident throughout Scripture. Man in biblical times lived closer to the soil. It was easier, perhaps, to consider work and faith as handmaidens in the same household.

With the coming of a highly complex industrial age, the

connection between work and faith became increasingly more difficult to maintain. As one writer has said, "It is easier to see God's gift in an ear of corn than in a steel rail." For most industrial work there are no rhythms of seasons. It is harder for a man to take pride in his own work and thus thank God for His creative guidance. The division of labor by which each person makes only a part of a finished product is one of the chief reasons for our age of plenty, but the spiritual and moral price we pay as a result is very high.

For millions, work is a drudgery, a grim necessity. Many hate their work every day of their lives and many find escapes in harmful ways to counterbalance the drudgery. Ask career counselors. Some estimate that as high as 90 percent of the labor market see themselves as *victims*, trapped in an unfulfilled daily round of work.

A Relevant Faith

Certainly if Christianity is going to be relevant, it must have something to say about this problem area. There is a Christian philosophy of the family, education, and history. Why not a Christian philosophy or theology of work?

One unfortunate development during the long history of the Christian church was the view during the Medieval period that there was a separation of the laity and the clergy. This difference between the sacred and secular callings still exists. In the architecture of early European cathedrals a screen separated the people from the priests because of the common view which held that working people had not been called of God in their tasks as the clergy had. Therefore, they had to worship apart.

Martin Luther saw the fallacy in this and courageously spoke out against it. He tore down this screen, and from him we get the idea of "vocational guidance." He said that man, in his worthier callings, is called just as surely as a man who is called to the priesthood or ministry.

Christianity, as both Paul and Luther demonstrated, has always provided a connection between work and worship. Men can dignify labor by doing ordinary things, but as redeemed persons. There lies the difference, and this is where the drudgery dissipates—God is in it. That means that every work bench in a plant is an altar! The Psalmist says, "And let the beauty of the Lord our God be upon us: and establish thou the work of our hands . . ." (Psalms 90:17). So you see, we can please the Lord by our work.

A Challenging Place to Work

The secular business world today is unquestionably difficult. It requires God's guidance in a special way. Temptations facing Christians are manifold; but they may be reduced to two.

First, we often work in an atmosphere of dishonesty. This is a major problem in the United States. It is not just an occasional theft here and there. Firms universally report large theft losses.

A major newspaper in the South carried a front-page story about a carpenter who bought a home and then furnished it with doors, windows, cabinets, and plumbing fixtures stolen from his employer.

Government reports indicate that employee dishonesty is extremely costly. In 1974, government experts estimated that firms lost 2 billion dollars in stolen tools, another 2 billion in pirated trade secrets, and 1.3 billion was appropriated for plant security. One shudders to think what the figure would be if it were not for plant guards and security.

Second, the business world has difficulties because of attitudinal problems. Theft is so commonplace. Few think anything of taking what they want without any qualms. An office girl, when caught stealing supplies from the office, was asked if she considered that wrong. "No, office supplies are just additional fringe benefits." She felt that she was not being paid enough, so she supplemented her income with secret fringe benefits. So what used to be considered stealing is now considered benefits owed by the boss.

Such an attitude on the part of adults is helping us to raise a new generation of thieves more adept than their fathers. In a recent national magazine there appeared a not-so-humorous cartoon. A young son was pictured being scolded by his father for stealing a pencil from school. The father indignantly asked, "What's the matter, son? Haven't I been bringing enough pencils home from the office?"

Let's Summarize

There are basically five truths which serve as guidelines for those who seriously believe what the Scriptures say about work and the attitudes and behavior that ought to go with it.

Choosing Our Work.   It is our feeling that a person's choice of work is a holy and wonderful thing, and that faith can provide a standard of reference. When one chooses his or her work it should not be merely in terms of secular or materialistic rewards or social standing. We need to become devoted to our daily work because God has instructed it. A spiritual sense and attitude toward work is heightened when we consider that God has a particular place or vocation where we can best serve Him.

Glorifying Worthy Work.   When honest, hard work is honored, even menial work can become significant. A man can stand what he is doing if he can see its larger meaning. Work that is totally pointless is unbearable.

There is no question that just about every job has a dull aspect, even the so-called Christian vocations. But every worthy job can be glorified by the conception of human service. If one does not see the hidden value and is not thinking in terms of the humanitarian aspect to his work, there will be little dignity.

A sociologist once interviewed workers in an American factory. He asked one worker, "What do you do?"

"I make C-28."

"What's C-28?"

"I don't know," was the reply.

The interviewer then wanted to know how long he had been working there.

"For ten years, sir," came the pathetic answer.

The Apostle Paul hinted at the need for dignity in one's work when he told the church at Thessalonica, ". . . work with your hands . . . so that you may command the respect of outsiders, and be dependent on nobody" (1 Thessalonians 4:11–12, RSV).

Bearing Up Under Difficult Work.   The Christian faith does not encourage any of us to look at the world through rose-colored glasses. The Christian realistically knows that there is much that is painful drudgery in his daily work. He must face cruel problems, work with disagreeable companions or boss, and face criticism or ridicule.

What must he do? He has to ask, "What can my faith do for me in this situation?" When he honestly searches out the answer, he will have an awareness that Christianity is centered in the Cross of Christ. Everyone who is misunderstood or hated can be helped by remembering that our Lord Jesus Christ was maligned. Remember, you are not alone. Many have walked such a path before you.

When you bear up under arduous labor, you can transform work into a meaningful experience. The word *patience* in the original Greek means "abiding under" difficulty. This is a very simple yet profound concept. With the right attitude and heart we can transcend all that is difficult. Think in terms of service. Make that office, factory, mill, or store a mission station. You'll have a new perspective.

Honesty Always the Best Policy.   We are to be honest with our employers and employees. This means honesty in time as well as commodities. Paul, in Romans 12:11, speaks out against sloth. The original word for *sloth* in New Testament Greek means *slowpoke.* On the job there is no room for deliberate slack or slowing down. Employers deserve an honest output. Proverbs 11:1 reads, "A false balance is abomination to the Lord: but a just weight is his delight." This puts it squarely up front. When you are inclined to cheat a little, God frowns upon it. It is an abomination to Him. The same Bible writer states, "Whatsoever thy hand findeth to do, do it with thy might . . ." (Ecclesiastes 9:10). In turn, employers must be equally open and honest in their dealings with those who work for them. This is always a two-way street.

In conclusion, we need to recognize that our work is ultimately for God. Regardless of who pays the salary, God is the one for whom we work.

Paul, in referring to work, states:

> Servants, be obedient to them that are your masters according to the flesh, with fear and trembling, in singleness of your heart, as unto Christ; Not with eyeservice, as menpleasers; but as the servants of Christ, doing the will of God from the heart; With good will doing service, as to the Lord, and not to men: Knowing that whatsoever good thing any man doeth, the same shall he receive of the Lord, whether he be bond or free.
>
> Ephesians 6:5–8

Timely words for a world so confused with unclear and confused values! When we work, we labor not only for the one who pays our salary, but for God as well.

4
Who, Me?

What you are to be you are now becoming.

HOW do you know if you're a workaholic? This is not an easy question to answer. Is it possible that *you* are one? Here are three general questions to ponder which may help to answer the question:

1. Do you find it difficult to become involved in activities other than your job?
2. Does *doing nothing* drive you up the wall?
3. How do you view hobbies or sports? Are they a *should* or a *must* instead of a *want to?*

If you answer yes to these questions, the chances are that you have a problem. If you're not yet a workaholic, you may well be heading in that direction.

As we have noted, work in itself is good. It is an extension of oneself. But when it becomes an excessive quality of life, it is changed from an extension to an escape. Rather than a delight it becomes a distortion.

Man has an unusual capacity to distort the good. Thirst is a basic drive for survival of the human organism. Yet drink (alcoholism) has become distorted so much in our time that it is undoubtedly America's severest domestic problem today. It has blighted millions of lives. It maims and kills. It destroys adult relationships and irreparably harms the children affected.

Fire is another of God's great gifts to man. It warms the

body and cooks our food. It drives great turbines and engines
for good. Yet man has perverted its use. Gunpowder and
weapons of war utilizing its energy have destroyed millions of
people since the Middle Ages.

Consider the alphabet. All twenty-six letters of our alphabet
are good. From those letters are formed beautiful four-letter
words such as *love, hope,* and *work.* Man's sinful nature can
take those same good letters and rearrange them to spell out
hateful and defamatory words which are meant for evil.

The workaholic perverts a good thing—work—into an evil.
He has misplaced values and distorted reality. Or, he may just
have gotten things mixed up somehow, as, for example, the
young minister who came to a church as a pastoral candidate.
He got carried away in his eloquence as he prayed for himself
in the Sunday-morning-service prayer: "And Lord, may the
one who has come to minister to this flock this morn be filled
with veal and zigor!"

However, as pointed out earlier, we must be careful not to
confuse work lovers with true work addicts. Mark Twain was a
work lover. Toward the end of his productive life he said he
hadn't done "a lick of work" in over fifty years. He wrote, "I
have always been able to gain my living without doing any
work; for the writing of books and magazine matter was always
play, not work. I enjoyed it; it was merely billiards to me."

The work lover works hard and long, but by choice. When
he wants to, he can stop. And, when he does, he can do it
without suffering withdrawal symptoms—grumpiness, emptiness, isolation, illness.

When a work addict goes on a vacation, he does so grudg-
ingly. It is not the natives but the tourists who are restless.

The work lover finds great satisfaction in his work because
to him it is almost his play. The true work addict cannot play,
so he works with mixed emotions. He has to keep at it because
he desperately needs the admiration of others, since so often
he does not approve of himself.

The healthiest people have a variety of sources or resources
for a full life. They are not locked in and they can go from one
activity to another without a feeling of guilt. They may be

bankers, but they are also husbands, parents, citizens, friends, churchgoers, art lovers, golfers, sports enthusiasts, and stamp collectors. If such a person loses his position, all his props for life are not knocked out from under him; his self-esteem is maintained.

What may we look for in distinguishing those who are better adjusted in life from those who manifest workaholic traits? There may seem to be almost as many different kinds of work- aholics in the world as there are people, but careful scrutiny will disclose that workaholics fall into certain types or patterns which are fairly discernable. Let's look at some of the most prominent types.

The "It Has to Be Done Right" Workaholic

This is the systematic workaholic. Watch for:

1. Almost everything done with complete abandonment
2. A perfectionist
3. Merciless demands upon himself
4. Intolerant of others' incompetence
5. Little elasticity or flexibility
6. Overcommitment to the organization
7. Highly skilled

Frequently as Phil walked down the hall of the medical center, he could be seen straightening the pictures hanging on the walls. Once inside his counselor's office he would invari- ably begin to count the stripes on the wall paneling. He re- ported that he got very little out of the church services. When asked the reason, he responded, "I find myself counting the organ pipes and the number of people in the choir, not once but repeatedly."

Phil's life could best be characterized by the word *orderli- ness*. He was a perfectionist. He was a superb dresser; he would never be caught in sloppy clothes. When he was in the army he would at times take three showers a day. Even his army fatigues would have to be pressed with a marked crease down the middle of the trousers. His personal belongings and effects were totally organized. His garage looked like the kitchen in the White House. Tools were hung symmetrically on the pegboard there. Nails, screws, nuts, washers arranged in the same size jars, all in a row. Every item was properly categorized and in its prescribed place.

Phil was a workaholic. He would stay late at night at the office. His reports had to be ready several days in advance. They were close to perfection. His supervisor dubbed Phil the best detail man in the organization.

The unfortunate part of this true story is that Phil expected everyone in his family to behave and operate in the same manner. His wife and children felt imprisoned. Each morning it was Phil's wife's job to awaken him, lay out his underwear and socks, choose his suit, shirt, and tie—which, of course, all had to match. Then it was her duty to precisely place his shaving equipment on the bathroom counter. As a part of the rigid morning schedule he had ordered, she was to run his bath water, to just the right temperature and level in the tub.

Hooked? You'd better believe it. The only reason he was in therapy was because his wife threatened to leave him. She couldn't cope with his absenteeism from home or his super-rigidity any longer.

This type of workaholic is the ultraperfectionist. He's addicted because he's cursed by conformity. Everything has to be done by the book. All the rules must be followed. He's locked into a system of his own choosing.

This type of workaholic usually can't make decisions. They are made for him. Alan N. Schoonmaker describes him perfectly:

> The conformist cannot tolerate the uncertainty of being alone or having to make his own decisions. He needs to lean on someone, because to him the freedom to make his own decision is not an opportunity but a threat. It means doubt, uncertainty, and anxiety. He therefore tries to escape from freedom by becoming like other people, by letting them tell him what to do. He lets them dictate his

work habits, his tastes, even his morals. He escapes from the anxiety of freedom to the security of conformity. But he also escapes from himself.

His conformity relieves the anxiety of uncertainty, but it costs him his identity. He is not a man in his own right, but a reflection of the people around him. He is a man without a core, a hollow man, standing for nothing and meaning nothing. His conformity relieves the uncertainty of not knowing what to do, but it creates a greater and more frightening uncertainty; he does not know who he is or what his life means. If he is absolutely without this knowledge, his life is intolerable and his anxiety is overwhelming.[1]

This type of workaholic is often extremely domineering. Leonard Cammer describes one in a work setting:

Uptight obsessive-compulsives from the corporation president down to the mailroom clerk, occupy space in every office. If you are a middle manager you embody the controlling superior, who demands total allegiance as a protection against your dormant insecurity. You set the ambiance, the schedules and the pace of the work.

You may consider it your duty to poke your nose into all established routine. Mail must go out at the time you designate (it always has); the files are to be cross-referenced your way (even if it makes no sense); you continually modify the form of letters (and when a ballup ensues, blame the stenographers); you create office schisms and power struggles (oblivious to them). One worker muttered: "When he walks in, the whole place gets crudded up." [2]

Because he is so organized and orderly he is a prize catch for any employer. He can do it all. His enthusiasm for data input goes on endlessly. He keeps a strict ledger for everything from personal income and expenditures to personal possessions. Everything is catalogued. He is a creature of method and routine because living has become a game of order for him.

But keeping records cannot continually help him to survive because they only lull him into a false sense of security, leaving him unable to deal adequately with the underlying stress that causes the maladaptive behavior in the first place. He becomes, thus, a prisoner within his own system of orderliness.

Leonard Cammer calls the perfectionist "the completer." [3] Such a person has the need to complete every task to its ultimate end. The carpenter matches every molding with infinite pains, the housepainter can't stand any streaks, the dressmaker has to make sure every stitch will hold permanently.

Cammer also says, "The problem with perfectionism is that it constantly threatens to choke off your adaptive comfort and make life a dance over hot coals between trepidation and panic." [4]

A White House assistant gave expression to the perfectionist philosophy when he said, "When I leave, I want to be confident I did everything I could have done." The workaholic perfectionist dies by this philosophy.

Another trait evident in this kind of workaholic is his sense of urgency of time. While trying to save time, this type of person will often become his own worst enemy. He will set deadlines for himself because he subconsciously believes that he can triumph over his archenemy, time.

"I don't have time to do that," or "There are just not enough hours in the day," are his pet sentences. They are more than stock phrases. The workaholic's vocabulary has a marked earnestness about it.

This type of person will often put himself under time pressure in order to beat the system or to drive himself to better systematize a project. Medical studies show that a person's blood pressure or cholesterol level may be determined just as much by what he feels under pressure as by what he eats. This, of course, makes the workaholic a prime candidate for heart disease.[5]

The perfectionist seldom realizes job satisfaction because his emphasis is often upon *faster* rather than *better,* although there can be a blending of the two. Time urgency can stifle the creative instinct and, very often, keenness of judgment.

One added feature about the systematic workaholic is that he must make work out of everything. Fun and games become a thing to work at. He constantly feels he is being judged—there's always a standard that has to be lived up to. If tennis is to be played, the fun quickly leaves, if it was there at all. Behind it all is the obsession that excellence has to be achieved. "Somebody may be watching." The game then disintegrates into work.

The "I Must Succeed" Workaholic

This is the pseudo workaholic. Things to watch for:

1. He's in a power struggle.
2. "The only way is up."
3. Competitiveness is the key word.
4. Egotistical
5. Power hungry
6. Can be a nice guy—"You scratch my back and I'll scratch yours."
7. Not so much interested in the company, but in moving up in the organization
8. An opportunist
9. Changes jobs often
10. Extremely aggressive; hard driver

Harold feels miserable on weekends. When at home he feels he has to be doing something all the time. In his late thirties, he became increasingly depressed. His wife, deeply concerned, called her minister who recommended that he seek professional counseling. Harold agreed, because he recognized the seriousness of his situation.

The first two sessions were spent talking about his work. He had a need to explain what a hard and effective worker he was. He explained it in great detail. Then about halfway through the third session he remarked to the therapist, "You know, I feel this is a waste of my time and yours. We haven't accomplished anything." The discerning counselor pointed this out as a problem. Harold was performance driven, expecting immediate answers. He wanted results—and now. Harold had never had that insight before. He began to see how his high performance standards were consuming him, influencing his whole life. He was wholly achievement oriented. Whether it was work or pleasure, he had to attain—now.

Harold could rarely leave the office right at quitting time. An unfinished project or task bugged him no end. He invariably stayed until it was completed. All the while, he was losing health, friends, and family. He had always considered himself a rational person, but now, due to depression, he was reacting to anxiety rather than facing reality. Somewhere, he had misplaced both his perspective and his values about work and life. Hal, as his friends knew him, was an egotist. It bothered him to be so open to another human being, such as his counselor, but it began paying off. The insight he was receiving was proving helpful and redemptive.

One of the most respected football coaches in the National Football League is noted for his intense dedication to his job. He once remarked to a friend that during the football season, especially, he allowed himself only three to four hours of sleep a night. He then added facetiously, "Everybody needs some leisure." He is a fierce competitor and has a drive toward success matched by few of his peers.

This type of person deludes himself into believing that he is sufficient to handle the extra load. "Sure, I'll give it the good old American try." Muhammad Ali, before his win over Leon Spinks, said it this way: "If you reach deep enough, you can always find it." We don't mean to imply that Ali is a workaholic, but his statement relates to the performance-driven person.

This type of workaholic has an insatiable drive to succeed. He will usually manifest it by a strong aggressiveness. Often he isn't concerned over who gets in his way. The person who is not so aggressively driven may also have a considerable amount of drive. We often forget this, but it is more balanced. The motivation of this latter type of person seems to steady him, providing more security, rather than irritating or producing symptoms hostile toward his environment.

It is unfortunate when a person caught up in the vise-like web of excessive competition transfers that drive to all aspects of life, not only to his business affairs but also to his leisure activities.

Dr. Meyer Friedman and his cardiologist coauthor, Dr. Ray H. Rosenman, divide the world into two working types. Hard-driving people are classified as Type A and low-pressure people as Type B. Both types can become workaholics, but in different ways.

Type A is characterized by excessive ambition and competitiveness. He also has hostility and feels greatly pressured by deadlines. Heart specialists say he is a prime candidate for a heart attack. In fact, he is two-to-three times as likely to have a premature attack as the Type B person.

The Type B workaholic is a civil-service type who loses himself in dull paperwork or other routine activities. He is more able to identify with the company he works for. He is more low-key.

Another unfortunate fact about the "I must succeed" workaholic is that he often does not get along as well with his peers and subordinates as he does with his superiors. This is oftentimes an unconscious thing because of his incessant drive to succeed. In that mold he feels the necessity to impress those to whom he reports or who are higher up the organization ladder. Often the fingers of those on the rungs below are crushed by the impelling climb of this workaholic. Perhaps the workaholic is not conscious of it, but it is evident to those with whom he closely relates.

It is like being named in one of the Howard Hughes' wills: you may not get a lot of money, but you sure get a lot of attention! The workaholic's peers are made very much aware of this and his subordinates resent the fact that he is constantly seeking to please his superiors and spends little time in meeting their felt needs.

One employee was overheard speaking of an overly aggressive status seeker, "One good thing about an egotist is that he says very little about other people."

We have a great deal to learn from our friends in the Third World in this matter of pressures upon people who continually strive for what they consider to be success. Ulcers are practically unknown in the Third World! The whole problem of the workaholic is not a recognized malady in developing and under-developed countries.

Because the hard-driving, competitive workaholic is over-committed to moving up the ladder of success, he rarely has time to develop close friendships. These people work long hours, frequently travel many miles across the country, and are eager to move up the organizational ladder. They often are willing to relocate every few years. Such activity prohibits them from making close friends.

There is usually a price to pay for promotions. At times, they destroy roots, since the new position makes it necessary to travel in uncharted and different circles. The high drive to move up often makes these individuals blind to the needs of other people. Obsessed with their own careers, production, and high-performance demands, they become oblivious to the world around them. They even become manipulators, using people to advance their own careers.

Frequently this kind of workaholic allows you to see only the tip of the iceberg. There is so much below the surface. Usually this type has an inferiority complex. A psychologist describes the person who has feelings of inadequacy by saying that a threat to a person's image creates anxiety. To build up the image, the person compares and competes with others. He continues:

> We wonder—for example—how much our associates earn, and we become very upset when we learn that someone is paid a salary higher than ours. We meet men with whom we went to school, and we try to find out whether we are "ahead" or not. We buy expensive cars, clothes, and homes, not because we need them to live comfortably, but to proclaim our success. We try to build up our departments, companies, communities, and coun-

try, and we·resent unfavorable comparisons. Within limits, this competition and comparison are relatively harmless (and they are certainly good for the economy), but some people overdo it.

Such people are so unsure of themselves that they have to keep pushing down their doubts. They may build themselves up by boasting, or surround themselves with yes-men, or always compete with others. They have to win in business, at golf, and at cards; their children must get the highest marks; their homes and cars must be the biggest and best. This degree of inadequacy feelings (some people call it an inferiority complex) is not caused by the competitive nature of our society. It is a basic part of their personality and will not be relieved by any amount—no matter how great—of success or reassurance. They carry their doubts and problems inside of themselves and will not feel comfortable until they obtain professional help.[6]

These kinds of people are the type who need to be continually pampered, at work and at home. They expect everyone in their life to instantly obey their orders.

The performance-driven person often is the tough customer. "I'm not paid to be a wallflower or to be popular. I'm here to get things moving, to produce, and if I have to push people around in the process, that's tough."

This individual will often display dominating and overly aggressive qualities which destroy relationships. At times these features may be useful and necessary, but they can likewise be most inappropriate. If a man bullies people, including his own family, he is defensive and has a problem. Such behavior will be nonproductive in many areas. This type of person needs to dominate, but it may eventually cost him his job and alienate his family.

On the other hand, the person who can be aggressive and assertive when the situation demands it is in control. His defenses then work properly for him. He can be tough on the job, but when he arrives home he can be tender and sensitive with his wife and children.

But the go-getter workaholic type is often the ideal worker—ambitious, hardworking, always willing to spend extra time on the job. He never complains about having too much to do. He will go anywhere the boss demands, with no questions asked. After all, he must drive to move ahead in his career. "I'm going to make it to the top and nothing is going to stand in my way!"

However, the go-getter type is not rational because he pays a high premium for his insurance to arrive at success, far too often costing him his family, health, satisfying work, and fruitful leisure time.

This person may appear confident, but, in actuality, he has little of it. He is forced to drive himself because he has so little faith in himself. He feels he must keep proving himself to others as well as to himself.

Furthermore his obsession to work makes him a slave. He lacks independence. He doesn't have the freedom to choose, since he's locked into a system—a system of his own making and choosing—because he is constantly forced to stay ahead of those who threaten him and his career. In seeking frantically to stay ahead he destroys the best things in life.

This type of person also lacks courage to be himself. Using work as a crutch to deaden the pain of anxiety, he is like an alcoholic who needs an escape. The principles are the same and the result often leads to the same dead end—isolation from the realities of life.

This individual sees his competitive edge as a strong motivating force in his life, one that literally keeps him going. His drive is further perpetuated by the culture which makes it virtuous to work hard in order to keep a step ahead of the next individual. So a veneer of virtue and goodness camouflages the inner self. This self-deception, which becomes a malignant cancer, weakens the total self, making a person less capable of dealing with real life. In some cases the resultant self-hate becomes so deep-seated that depression becomes the norm and even suicide may be contemplated.

Bear in mind that the performance-driven workaholic is often unsatisfied with his work. Because he is success oriented he may take a position which he does not especially enjoy. If a company offers him more money, he will take that job, and will then pride himself in the prestige that goes with it. He will explain his actions by saying, "I took the job because it meant that I might move ahead faster."

Look for these attributes of the "power men": autocratic, results oriented, insensitive, intolerant, direct, dominant, competitive, egocentric, inflexible, determined, aggressive. The achiever workaholic is task oriented, goal oriented (short range), analytical, candid, knowledgeable, fact oriented, independent, impatient. As a manipulator, he often is one who uses people. He is an opportunist—persuasive, calculating, self-serving, inquisitive, subtle, and evasive.

The "I Have to Get Away From It All" Workaholic

This is the isolated workaholic. Things to watch for:

1. An escape artist
2. Conscientious
3. A loner
4. Does not need people
5. Afraid to get too close to people
6. Response to people at work often cool
7. Seems bored with life in general
8. Deep inferiority complex
9. Seldom laughs heartily
10. A killjoy
11. Job is a substitute for all other relationships
12. Often has deep marriage conflicts

Jeffrey is a quiet man. In a counseling session his wife said, "You never know he's around." He is soft-spoken; he has never been in any kind of trouble. His boss reports that he never has to worry about him: "He always does an exceptional job. The work gets done. It may be done at his own pace, but I can always count on him to do superior work."

Jeffrey has communicated for several months in therapy that he cannot see the importance of being with people while at work. "During my lunch hour, I usually stay at my desk to eat my sandwich. Sometimes I will go down to the lunchroom and sit in a corner with a book under my nose while eating a package of pretzels and drinking a soft drink. What's the big deal?" he says. "Everyone looks at me thinking I'm a great success."

On the job, Jeffrey does superb work. As a husband and father, he is a failure. Witness his own words: "I thought if I made it on the job, everything else would fall into place." This was the reason which explains why his wife had filed for a divorce.

In counseling, the subject of sex came up. Jeffrey admitted never openly displaying much emotion toward his wife or daughters. "Sexually, I guess I'm dead inside. I would never do any disgusting things like speak love words with romantic metaphors. I've always been repulsed, for some reason, by erotic thoughts or fantasies. They're a sign of weakness. After all, sex is just fulfilling a biological urge, a body function. That's all."

Jeffrey began to see, as the veil was removed from his eyes by the therapist, that intimacy was out of the question because he was afraid to expose his inner feelings, afraid to let go. He's a genuine workaholic, using his work as a means to keep his distance. "People like me to be busy; they commend me for my accomplishments."

This common type of workaholic needs to work excessively because he uses it as a crutch to escape anxiety and other people. He's the loner type. He may work hard and be very conscientious, but he is often a very poor staff person. He rarely can stand criticism. He does not welcome feedback from his peers. He may not be nasty or antisocial; he just wants to be left alone.

"I can think better when I'm left alone," is his rationale. "I don't have time for a lot of chitchat. It's a waste of time." He doesn't take coffee breaks. Vacations are a rarity. This type of workaholic does not need people. He doesn't want to become involved. Usually it's because he's afraid of hurt or rejection. He more often than not is out of touch with his or others' emotions.

His aloofness is his defensive barrier or protection. This makes him tone-deaf to the feelings of others, since he is turned inward. To him this is rational behavior, but it is not rewarding because he becomes completely isolated from society. You seldom get a warm, firm handshake from him.

He may genuinely desire close personal relationships, but he rationalizes that he really doesn't need people. He's actually afraid to get too near, so he remains uninvolved with people and overcommitted to the impersonal world of work.

This type of workaholic finds his addiction to work very difficult to shake because it works for him, at least for a time, until someone, perhaps his wife, begins to react. It is tough to shake because it becomes an escape from the problems of life and family tensions. It becomes a device to overcome inferiority complexes. It also is an escape from oneself and even from God.

The isolated workaholic seldom achieves pleasure from activities that should be fun. He seemingly has no time for such frivolities because his time is consumed avoiding what he considers a waste of time.

Usually this type of person has no conscious idea of the energy and time devoted to his self-hate which makes him refrain from enjoyment. Many such persons have difficulties in achieving a sexually fulfilled life.

A client came to a counselor complaining of frequent depressions. Each such period drove him to dig in more at his work, to lose himself in his job as he described it. He reported that each time he went through such a time of depression, he noticed difficulty in achieving orgasm with his wife. At the exact moment, worrisome thoughts would enter his mind about a task he would need to do the following day at work or some current problem he faced in the office. Such a preoccupation then blocked the pleasurable impulses. Later in therapy he even began to determine before getting involved sexually if he would go through the complete satisfying experience. Of course he never did, because he was unable to act spontaneously.

Bill, without knowing it, had been a killjoy for years, believing himself to be unworthy of pleasure. What he was doing was making an unconscious pact with his self-hate, giving up pleasure in payment for relief from depression and other self-hate mechanisms. It worked for a while, until he began to realize that life was beginning to pass him by.

Wayne Oates describes this type of workaholic:

> The typical workaholic is as averse to admitting his dependent needs as is the alcoholic. As long as he has his work, he does not "need" anybody—he has power, place and things. But when he shucks off the role of the self-sufficient one as he closes the office door or leaves the factory, he slams head-on into himself as the dependent one.[7]

This kind of workaholic manifests his basic personality problem wherever he goes. He usually does not pretend to be one person in one setting and another someplace else.

> A man is not one person at home and a different person at his work, he is one and the same man. He projects his personal worries, frustrations and fears on to his workplace, and vice versa from workplace to home.[8]

The isolated workaholic is a pathetic figure, cut off from people, alone, left to fight all his battles without help. His job becomes his only safety zone.

The "I Need Their Approval" Workaholic

This is the pacifist workaholic. Things to watch for:

1. An around-the-clock man
2. Amenable and seldom shows anger
3. Fear of failure because of low self-esteem
4. Jovial
5. Takes moonlighting jobs
6. A status seeker
7. Always wants a prestigious title
8. Company oriented
9. A yes-man and backslapper

10. Deep inferiority complex
11. Apologetic

Arnold is a forty-eight-year-old production-control manager for a large automotive plant. He has five hundred employees under his supervision.

One day there came an emergency call to a counselor. Arnold's wife was on the other end, pleading with the therapist, "Please, please, my husband has to see someone right away."

Arnold shuffled into the therapist's office at the appointed time, slumped on the sofa and began crying uncontrollably. After a few minutes he was able to talk. "For twenty-four years I've dedicated myself completely to my job. I can't take it anymore. I'm coming apart. Everything, even little things, get to me. I can't sleep, I can't eat. I do the best that I can, but I'm so afraid to make a mistake."

Arnold was suffering from severe mental torment and physical problems which were causing great pain. During that first session he described the feelings as being like a giant band ever tightening around his chest area, severe pounding of his heart, tingling in his arms. He had been to a cardiologist a week earlier. His heart was in solid shape.

Arnold, in the counselor's presence, was experiencing a severe anxiety attack. As he spoke, one could sense the tension. He bit down on his teeth with great intensity. Every cell in his body seemed to be pulsating with tension. He began to roughly scratch his legs. They felt as if they were on fire, he reported.

This man was a workaholic. "I'm always doing, doing, doing; working through my lunch hours. When I get home I can't turn loose of it. My wife's fed up with me. I can't handle it."

Another competent man has bit the dust. All because he was painfully afraid of making a mistake, revealing his humanness.

One of the basic drives of the human personality is the desire for approval. Without good strokes a person feels useless.

Most of us want the satisfaction that comes from being accepted and recognized as people of worth by our friends and work associates. Money is only a small part of this social recognition. The way we are greeted by our boss, being asked to help a newcomer, being asked to keep an eye on a difficult operation, being given a job requiring special skill—all of these are acts of social recognition. They tell us how we stand in our work group. We all want tangible evidence of our social importance.[9]

The pacifist workaholic becomes one because his self-esteem is low, so he tries to live up to an image which places him in a good light among his peers.

Johnny Carson, talented TV personality, has been quoted as saying, "I am driven to work as much as I do because I please people and I need to continue pleasing them."

With all types of workaholics, we cannot be certain what the deep underlying anxiety or tension is that drives such people to excessive work, unless it is revealed. But one thing is sure: all use overwork as a tactic to run away from feelings of inadequacy. The workaholic who constantly needs approval thinks very poorly of himself. Therefore, he works to relieve the feelings of guilt, hurt, or failure. Work and status become a means of removing self-doubt. Because of hidden insecurities, this type of person becomes a compulsive worker.

The workaholic's ego must continually be reinforced with the tangible results seen in work achievement. He needs to be affirmed by the symbols of money, awards, trophies, production figures, and constant praise for achievement. These become substitutes for love for its own sake.

In seeking approval the individual's feeling about himself is less important than the opinion others hold about him. Constantly searching for approbation, he becomes overburdened and oftentimes intensely discouraged with himself.

The unfortunate thing for the pacifist workaholic is that he ends up not knowing who he is because he becomes subject to everyone else's whims and fancies.

This kind of workaholic really feels more secure when working. He or she has a compulsive need to work, like a famous ballerina who said, "I may not be able to work tomorrow. It's not that applause that I like—it's the fact that I am working."

The "I Have to Better My Lot in Life" Workaholic

This is the situational workaholic. Things to watch for:

1. Works out of necessity
2. Economically driven
3. Materialistic
4. Prestige needs of his wife and family
5. "Keep up with the Joneses" syndrome
6. Job security not all that great
7. May hold down several jobs
8. A contempt for others
9. Bored with life in general
10. Measures success in terms of salary
11. Usually quite an unhappy person

Dr. Theodore I. Rubin relates a pertinent story describing this type of workaholic:

I recall seeing a patient who earned fifteen thousand dollars a year. He told me at the time that earning twenty-five thousand a year "would seem like Heaven" to him. I warned him, to no avail, of the many other kinds of exorbitant goals he harbored and told him that unless his complete outlook changed he would never feel that he earned enough.

Within a relatively short time his earnings increased enormously. But his quick appreciation for these rapid increases turned as rapidly to contempt. His living expenses soared with his income and so did his appetite for all kinds of things he never knew he needed before. These included very high insurance policies, a larger house, better clothes, private schools for his children and many more of "the good things of life."

When he was earning twenty-five thousand dollars a year he told me that he really was only feeling the satisfaction that came of earning five thousand a year. This was considerably less satisfaction than he got from the fifteen thousand he earned when he first came to see me. This was so, he told me, because it now cost him "twenty thousand-plus a year just to get by my basic needs." This left less than five thousand to do what he wanted with. He was also angry because he had to pay so much in taxes. I reminded him that he once told me that he would "love to earn enough money so as to have to pay plenty of taxes. I should only be in that position."

He went on to earn over a hundred thousand and his financial and emotional condition became even worse. My intervention became almost negligible because while his earning ability brought less and less satisfaction, it nevertheless increased his very real self-hate and arrogance. He was loathe to investigate any possibility of examining standards and expectations, let alone lowering them. He was caught in a self-grinding, ever-escalating goal enterprise, which was utterly ruthless in its pressure on him. To complicate matters the expectations he had of his children were being thwarted in some ways by his affluence, too. His daughter had taken up with a private-school crowd that experimented with drugs. He really had believed that money and affluence would prevent such things, that if he gave his children the best of everything they would be immune to "crummy things." [10]

Rubin relates that this patient finally had a heart attack from which, fortunately, he recovered. He began to evaluate his standards, goals, and expectations and had to relearn the value of enjoying life—appreciating friends, a sunset, or taking a walk.

Regretfully, it took a heart attack to bring about such change. Think of the pain which could have been avoided if this man had not allowed self-hate to consume him. The author goes on to state that in therapy the man did not want to hear about other people because he was identifying more with his own negative self and with rejection. He viewed other people with contempt.

The workaholic is obsessed with getting things done. This is also transferred into the accumulation of material objects. As one observer has put it, squirrels accumulate nuts and bees honey, but they do so strictly for utilitarian purposes. When winter comes they instinctively have forfended hunger. They don't do it simply for the pleasure of adding to what they already possess.

Because the situational workaholic interprets success with dollars and time units, he may have a strong temptation to hoard whatever he can get his hands on. He overvalues quantity above quality.

His absorption with numbers in terms of time and dollars gives him tunnel vision, so that the rest of life has this interpretative quality about it. He is left with fewer responses to life choices.

Money represents many different things to different people. A father once said to his daughter's suitor who was unable to hold a job down and make any money, "My daughter says you have that certain something; I wish you had something certain." A young actor who admits to being a workaholic recently said, "I just want to be different; it costs money to be different these days."

In our American culture we are taken up with the need to survive financially. Just to make ends meet today is a colossal task, but there is an added appeal about the good life. This compounds the problem for today's worker who feels the pressure. Erwin Smigel touches on this when he says:

> There is a built-in cumulativeness about many consumer goods; the house can always be added to or improved; a car is a standing invitation to travel and to evenings out on the town; a television set, an invitational mirror of the good life.[11]

One of the major causes behind the workaholic's self-driven need for things is the fact that he is often bored with life. Typical statements are, "I'm so bored, I might as well keep my mind occupied through my work"; and, "If I only had more money, I wouldn't be so bored all the time."

One workaholic professed that his only interest in life was his business and making more money. About the only time he ever expressed joy of any kind was when his bank balance increased.

When this was pointed out to him he told a sad story about his upbringing. Whenever he began to build model airplanes or enjoy sports, his father would sharply criticize him for wasting valuable time and money. "Son, your interests in life should be higher. You should be out working; money is the only thing that talks." These were the messages his father repeatedly gave him. This man grew into adulthood enveloped in the tyranny of the *should*'s to the degree that he disliked any aspect of himself that sought pleasure or relaxing pursuits.

Through therapy he was made to see that his boyhood interests were not really dead, and he was later helped to develop other areas of his life. It had appeared that the only thing that mattered was the world of commerce. Money had actually little to do with it. Everything else in life had lost perspective because it was considered to be nonimportant, unfulfilling, or unproductive. Thus, the complaint of boredom.

A wife reported that she never saw her husband since he started a business. She knew there would be long hours and loneliness, but she felt it had gone on too long and was far out of proportion. Her husband was a stranger to their children.

This kind of a situation demands special understanding on the part of the family. Most of the worthwhile adventures in life require certain kinds of sacrifices. A wife must realize that this is only a temporary circumstance. Her husband needs the extra time to get the business off the ground.

In such an instance, the wife will have to learn to submerge some of her personal wants beneath the overall ultimate objectives she and her husband have set for the family. In most cases the husband is not acting irresponsibly.

Because the business is "ours," the problem must be confronted with an "it's ours to work out together" attitude. This is the only way around it. A constantly carping wife may only add fuel to the existent tensions and create more guilt for the husband who may feel caught in the middle.

Jay Kesler, in one of his fine books, talks about an Air Force study that has a bearing on this topic.

> The Air Force did a study a few years ago concerning why certain Air Force children go bad and why certain Air Force children seem to be happy. It relates mostly to how the mother in the marriage feels about her husband's work. Is she always complaining? If she is, the children tend to grow up hating the Air Force, and they often rebel against their parents.[12]

The point is well taken. In a situation where a man is forced to make a go of it in the financial support of his family, the most important consideration for his wife is to back off from criticism. He needs all the support he can get.

The man or woman who lives with the fantasy that money solves everything is in deep trouble. He or she sees the world mainly in economic terms and as a consequence closes off options to live a full, social, emotional, and spiritually enriched life. Each stunts his own growth potential, becoming a partial person, and deprives himself of human satisfaction in the fullest sense.

Like all addictive behavior, the problem of workaholism sneaks up on a person. Many known addicts won't admit that their problem is serious. Many workaholics are what some psychologists are calling *maze-dull.*

Dr. Eugene Jennings, a psychologist and management professor at Michigan State University, in a newspaper article, lists several qualities that mark the maze-dull personality. Some of these characteristics are often seen in workaholics:

First, a vast ego; an idealized notion of self. This is the essential character trait that hides the imminence of trouble. Because of his isolation, the workaholic is guilty of the sin of presumption. He presumes that things are all right or there is more power to the office than there is; and, he presumes that his personal power is greater than it really is. The organization can't exist without him.

Second, inward-oriented intelligence. Maze-dull people seek answers within. They immerse themselves in every detail. They are meticulous: they read incessantly. They do not trust others. Such behavior keeps them involved in trivia and prevents them from making the big decisions that can change the course of events. It prevents them from building a team, from tapping available wisdom.

Third, a tendency toward ideas and programs almost to the exclusion of people. They believe a bright idea, when enunciated, should be convincing in itself. They do not feel they need to get involved in interaction with others to get appropriate feedback.

Fourth, intention versus consequences. They believe that good consequences follow good intentions. They fail to anticipate the consequences of their own behavior. Nearly all workaholics have their heads in the sand on this one. They seem oblivious to the havoc around them which is created by their avoidance and isolation. Faced with consequences other than those they foresee or feel are justified, they either cave in or become like a bull in a china shop.

In our discussion of the five major types of workaholics, there are common elements seen in all of them. One may be tempted to oversimplify. The point is, if your work habits are directing you toward a dead end, with yourself or with other people, it is now time to take a personal inventory!

It is certainly not our purpose to lay a guilt trip on anyone unnecessarily. Some symptoms which are seen in the workaholic may, in themselves, be good. Indeed every successful person will have some of the attributes cited, such as being success or achievement oriented, possessing great skills, having a strong commitment to an organization, setting standards of excellence, and so forth. However, it is important to know when they are being overused to cause behavior that is not in keeping with the laws of mental health and healthy interpersonal relations.

Under the control of God's power in one's life, these good personality characteristics can be redemptive and may be used for His glory.

Work addiction is like any other addictive behavior. In the early stages no one even notices. It's like an alcoholic. You find only about 3 percent who end up on skid row. The rest are "up-and-outers." They admit only to being social drinkers.

Slowly the process of erosion begins to consume the workaholic victim. At first the individual professes to truly enjoy his work. There may even be a genuine excitement about it. Socially, he will warmly talk about the job, its challenges and meaning. The swapping of stories about the job is commonplace. He may not even be aware of imminent danger, letting the best things in life escape him—his values, his family, his friends.

5

It's a Family Affair

A workaholic's race toward success may be an attempt to escape family responsibilities.

JOHN is a man in his mid-thirties. Already he's working on his fourth marriage. He boasts that he loves 'em and leaves 'em. His longest marriage is the current one, going on four years. But it's in deep trouble. One thing about John is that he's never wrong, to listen to him. He admits to working fourteen to sixteen hours, six days a week, for the past fifteen years. He drives a bus for a city-transportation company during the day. At night he hurries home, takes a shower, eats in about fifteen minutes, and then dashes off to his second job as a night cook at a local restaurant.

If the traffic has flowed well on the way home from work and his wife has the meal ready, he may (and again may not) spend ten or fifteen minutes an evening with his three children. It's getting so they don't want to spend time with him. His wife reports they never ask about their father. He's practically a stranger in their midst.

John doesn't know it, but he's about ready to lose his present wife. She can't take it any longer. He's never around to share the problems of the children. The discipline is left up to her. What's more, they never socialize and have few friends.

Sue, his wife, is outgoing, personable. She knew before they were married that John was obsessed with work. They discussed it. But she thought she could make John realize the importance of family responsibilities. She was going to be his savior. In her fantasy, there were high hopes, now turning to ashes. To add to the difficulty, she no longer has much resource left to cope with all the burdens. Her migraines are getting increasingly severe and she suspects colitis or some type of digestive problem.

John's behavior is responsible for destroying a family. It is typical of many other workaholics.

There's More Than Meets the Eye

We hear a great deal today about the causes of breakup of marriage in our society—the lure of sex in mass media, the materialism push, and the glamorization of the pursuit of mere pleasure. We live in a playboy world.

The Christian ethic of faithful and abiding relationships is under great attack by this philosophy of hedonism which makes pleasure the chief goal in life. This has led to the "new morality," which isn't new at all. It's as old as mankind itself. Early civilizations were destroyed because of the undermining of fidelity and sobriety in this respect.

Sex, however, is but one factor that plays havoc with relationships in our society. The addiction to work is likewise a form of infidelity on the part of one partner. It also creates bitter feelings of estrangement, loneliness, jealousy, hurt, anger, and frustration. A partner has gone after another "lover." He wishes to spend more time with work than he does with his spouse and family. The feelings of tension and personal hurt may not be as intense as other factors, but the result is the same, estrangement and a gnawing aloneness on the part of the left-out spouse.

Without question, a major reason for the rising divorce rate in this country is the long hours spent on the job. The wife is the one who is hurt more when her husband travels or devotes an inordinate amount of time at work. Some wives go along with the problem. Others begin to react strongly, especially when children are involved. The workaholic is frequently caught in the middle. He has powerful demands upon him at work and he may have an extremely unhappy wife at home.

He can't cope with both, so he will often turn inward and become more of an isolate.

It is obvious that at times we all probably spend too long a period and too many hours on the job. The real problem arises when it seems to be all the time, or at least a majority of the time. In either case, we must recognize that the family suffers!

These conflicts create much anxiety. Many wives grow weary of long hours alone and resentments begin to build. They begin to demand more affection and companionship. Many start nagging and they soon begin to dread asking that haunting question, "Are you working again tonight?"

Some wives, of course, say little, but they may be good candidates for numerous trips to the doctor's office with all sorts of psychosomatic ills. Their loneliness, resentment, and jealousy of their husband's work begin to take their toll.

The workaholic husband in many cases makes no great personal investment in his family. As a result, the domestic life of a workaholic is frequently in trouble. (In some interesting cases, addicts marry each other and go on through life, each doing his or her own thing!)

More typically, the wife is not an addict. With the passage of time her patience begins to wear thin and growing resentment becomes the rule rather than the exception. The workaholic not only has the problem of proper time spent with the family, but because of his emotional hang-up he often expects his wife and children to be robotlike perfectionists. Usually he isn't the type to help around the house, but he typically may poke his nose into the household affairs, directing everybody in the proper way of doing things, even cooking and housework. He is so preoccupied with his own work goals he lacks sensitivity to the needs of those in his family.

Vacations can be bummers for workaholics and their families. Indeed, one who suspects he may be becoming psychologically addicted to his work should ask whether he can readily unwind over a weekend or during a vacation. How often we hear of wives who report vacations as utter failures. There was one such wife who finally got her husband to take

her on a holiday for the first time in many years, only to find
that he made it miserable for everyone. He constantly had to
phone his office; he simply couldn't relax. After just three days
away, the whole family was more than ready to return home.

When a family problem exists, it seems that the solution for
the workaholic is to add more work, thereby shortening the
already burdened amount of time he has to spend with them.
Wayne Oates provides insight into the disillusioned thinking
of such a person:

> . . . the addition of more work will both allow him to
> get away from his family and give him a pious reason for
> doing so. If they only appreciated him more, were not so
> extravagant, were not so lazy, and knew the importance of
> work, then the family would not have as many problems
> as it has.[1]

There is no question that our hard-driving commercial
world is taking a vast toll on marriages. At one time, if a man
experienced a divorce it was felt he was unfit for a company—
the philosophy being that if he could not take care of problems
at home, he couldn't properly take care of a job within the
company.

Today there seems to be an incredible new mood pervading
the work scene. An executive with a large corporation in the
Midwest expressed it to a colleague in this way: "A man who
gets divorced now is probably in a better position to get advanced upward. It shows that his loyalty is not to his wife and
family but to his company, which he places first and above
them."

This will be a sad commentary on our present generation if
this philosophy is universally adopted in the business world.

A Word to Women

Obviously, our women readers will identify with many of
the problems and characteristics related to the work trap as
they will sense some of the same patterns. But there may be
additional insights as we consider women's roles in our society. Women today represent a large force in our world. They
control a good deal of the wealth of our society. Furthermore,

one of three wives in our country is working outside the home. Many of them work not by choice but to pay the bills! This in itself can and does cause much stress on the American home.

Women continue to enter the labor market in ever-increasing numbers. The American Business Women's Association claims there are approximately thirty-seven million working women. According to a recent Associated Press report, the U. S. Labor Department has stated that in September 1978 more than 50 percent of the American labor market was comprised of women.[2]

Many women become addicted to their work because of their own compulsive need to feel important and to have control over themselves or others. Some actually report that they work so hard and diligently because of the sense of power they derive from being on the *inside* of an organization. The following quote states the case well:

> She will work at all hours, on Saturdays, Sundays, and holidays. She will forgo vacations for four or five years in succession. She will baby-sit for an executive free of charge. She will travel all night to be the secretary at a secret session of executives. She will help the boss's wife Christmas shop, and prepare their personal Christmas cards at night after she gets home. She will accept all sorts of insults, low pay, and a total lack of appreciation. All of this in return for one thing—to know everything that is going to happen before anyone else does, and to know why it happened, straight from the horse's mouth. Her inner supposition, her fantasy, is that such knowledge is power, actual or potential. In brief, the sexual and parental dimensions of the secretary's relationship to her boss have been greatly overemphasized. The power dimensions have been ignored. The desire for power is fuel to work compulsions in women and makes dyed-in-the-wool workaholics of them.[3]

The Houseproud Wife

You've heard it rightly said, "Man's work is from sun to sun, but a woman's work is never done." This proverb assumes that

women must always work. The tragedy is that husbands and
children allow it to happen. Indeed, a housewife can be a
workaholic. She may insist on doing so much that her children
never learn everyday chores or household skills. The
daughters of such women often grow up not knowing how to
cook, sew, or do housework. They don't learn how to decorate
either cakes or the home in an acceptable way.

It is true there are many laborsaving devices which have
resulted from the scientific technology of our day. But these
conveniences merely shift the areas of work for the
homemaker rather than decrease it. They also increase the
need for money to operate them all. This problem is described
this way:

> She spends much of her time negotiating with repair
> people to keep gadgets in working order. She spends a
> large portion of her day chauffeuring around her family,
> who a generation ago would have walked or used public
> transportation or car pools. With the telephone in the
> home, she spends considerable amounts of time sending
> and receiving messages. She is the "control tower"
> operator of a home that is more like an airport than a
> private abode. Everybody lands and departs on schedules
> which require almost computer-like mastery of detail to
> synchronize . . . she is also custodian of charge accounts
> and checking accounts. This in itself calls for infinite pa-
> tience and attention to detail . . . . Add to this the re-
> sponsibilities for entertainment, both personal and offi-
> cial . . . . The workaholic housewife is an example of
> perpetual motion. Her favorite phrase is: "Let me do it."
> When a visiting friend, relative, or passing stranger says
> "May I do that?" she firmly says, "No," and means it. She
> generally spurns domestic help, insisting adamantly that
> she would rather do it herself. She, too, is a perfectionist.
> No one can do her work right but herself.[4]

Under such circumstances as these the housewife can indeed become addicted to her work to the exclusion of more
important values.

Work As an Avoidance?

The overworked woman may toil all day so she has little energy left over for her husband. It is often a means, as well, of avoiding sexual intimacy. The headache excuse probably has run its course. Work now becomes the way to get off the hook, as it were. One such woman told her friends, "Who needs sex anyway? I've been married for many years. I only let my husband near me once a month, if then. But I do like to be held." Yet her friends readily noted how involved she was in everything else in the home and community.

Means of Control?

Like her male counterpart, the workaholic woman who is married compulsively feels she must control her husband and the home. And, if reminded that she wears the trousers in the home, comes the reply, "I'd never think of it." She will, however, keep a constant surveillance on her family. Every minute has to be accounted for.

Leonard Cammer describes this type of woman further:

> She grasps into her own hands the control of the man upon which the guarantees of her security are found and emasculates him. While she may hunger at times for affection, her anxieties dictate that only her possessions and the enslavement of those around her offer safe destiny.
>
> She does not want the man. She despises him. Equally, she scorns the subjective reality of her marriage. Solely, it is the facade that counts. In her words, "I'm interested only in the impression on the popular mind and the respect of the community we have to live in!"
>
> In suppressing her husband, she reinforces her dominance and presents him instead with a beautiful and orderly home as cold and sterile as herself. But the cat's paw does not remain forever quiescent. Mr. _____, disillusioned by the vital deficiencies of his marriage and unable to accept them, at last leaves his controlling wife and her "home." [5]

You know what your husband thinks about it all? "Mrs. Perfection, I'd sure like to bring some of the boys from the office home some time on a spur-of-the-moment impulse. No, I can't do that. You would have to know days in advance. If only you'd let go once in a while. You're always hassling the kids to pick up their messes, and me—I feel imprisoned in my own house. I wish you were like our neighbor's wife. Joe can eat a bag of potato chips in the living room without her coming all unglued."

If you are like this, you are making too great a sacrifice to maintain your high standards. You deny your husband the use of his home as his castle, for his social wants. The trade-off with your children may be more devastating. You substitute a germ-free home and orderliness for empathy and fondness. Sure, people admire you for your well-kept home. But others are probably saying, "Who needs that? She works like a horse." She's the woman who, upon preparing for guests, is compelled to clean the house from top to bottom. Leonard Cammer describes this kind of workaholic wife as follows:

> Your energy as you tackle your household each day is a marvel. You miss nothing and make it all look so easy. The cleaning woman never does the kitchen "right" so you take it on yourself. If asked, "What about the plumber? Are you right behind him making sure that he picks up every scrap of refuse that he drops?" you answer simply, "I don't like the plumber there at all."
>
> One sighs for you, locked into your pathetic world of choredom, no songs of delight, words and music only of your things and their museum status. You are the vintage obsessive-compulsive perfectionist whose career is your home with its voice directing: "Keep me always in perfect alphabetical order." [6]

There are many uptight women who will give up the pleasures of life for the tyranny of their scheduled pressures. They may find it hard to laugh, rejoice, or love. One workaholic

woman reported to her doctor that she would only take a three-
or four-minute bath. Duty demanded that she keep pushing
on.

Medal for Merit. "First prize of show" for houseproud
goes to you for your valiant efforts in protecting your
oriental rug to the death. Grimly, you have trained your
dog to wipe its four feet on a special mat at the door, and to
patter on hind legs near the walls on the bare floor, then
down, rest, patter—down, rest, patter—until it reaches its
own turf in the house. Poor dog. Poor you. The only win-
ner here is the rug.[7]

Little Flexibility?

Then there is what Cammer calls the "systems woman."
Here is a classic type of workaholic woman. She's the kind
who thoroughly enjoys a computerized psyche. "I love working in the accounts office. We have computers and everything
always comes out to the penny. It's so satisfying." [8]

When at home, this kind of woman is tied down to lists.
Everything is planned with no allowance for flexibility.
Whether it's sewing, shopping, doing laundry, it must be done
in precise order. And, in the preparation, no one better be in
the way to derail the express!

Then there's the martyr type. When there's company, this
little woman demands that no one go to the kitchen to help
clean up the dinner dishes. She's going to do it all, so company
and family can relax in comfort and fully enjoy the evening.
But listen to her the next day complain about all the work.
"You kids make me so mad. No one offered to even pick up a
dish and put it in the dishwasher." For days you hear the
endless complaint about how much work she had to do when
company came to dinner.

Cammer illustrates the obsessive-compulsive woman in this
insightful way:

You are the O-C woman who recently said on the telephone: "I'm going to let it all hang out. You wouldn't

believe it, but here I am with a breaking back, waiting on my husband hand and foot, who's in bed with the flu, and running between him and my son in the other room, who also has a fever. And the maid away. My mother came to help but I sent her home because I had the trays and medicines all organized. It was my job to get my family well. All I could do was suffer through it, even with my back killing me. We're not exactly poor and it's ridiculous for a woman in my position to be drudging like this . . . . No one would ever do it for me. But I have to think of my conscience. When it's all over, everyone will be fine except me. Will anyone ever appreciate it? Never." [9]

The martyr-type woman will always let her family know about home care. She will fuss a great deal about the messes in the house. But she won't give orders or direction and she won't train her family to pick up. She hates to have to do the work, but at the same time, her compulsion is born out of a deep neurotic need for approval.

Thus, the house becomes an end in itself. No one can relax and it becomes a devastating environment in which it is impossible to raise happy, well-adjusted children.

Those women who do not comprise a part of the outside-the-home labor force become a target for all kinds of enterprises which seek to utilize their time. Most of them are legitimate services such as the church, fund-raising drives, school or institutional volunteer work, and so forth. Such a housewife who gets involved must be careful of overcommitment to such activities. She is in danger of becoming a workaholic to the exclusion of home, husband, and children.

One husband reported with a note of dismay that his wife "knows everything and does everything." She needs to establish her priorities just as assuredly as any man who sits in an office all day and is faced with decisions that demand his time.

Women, like men, have to find solutions for nonproductive areas of their lives. Feelings of inadequacy or nonacceptance, as well as the need for approval, should be explored and changed if they contribute to work addiction. Then determine to alter your life by changing the pace. Wayne Oates suggests that you should have fun—go with a friend to lunch, visit the hairdresser, join a health club, go window-shopping, or simply find a place with a beautiful view and just sit and do nothing. Learn from a pregnant woman, as Oates further suggests:

> When the pregnant woman is sitting still, doing nothing, she is accomplishing everything. The mystery of the physiology of a woman is a symbol of the creativity of the capacity to cooperate with rather than to try to force nature. The silent wisdom of the body teaches the relationship between work and rest, growth and repose, effort and release. A rhythm of being is inherent that in the sophistication of our civilization and artificiality we have either not learned consciously or have forgotten. It can be learned; it can be remembered; it can be taught. The symbolism of the "work" of the birth process is a silent antithesis to the frenetic activity of the workaholic. For that reason this symbolism is the parable that both male and female workaholics have to learn in order to be genuinely productive and at peace with oneself at one and the same time.[10]

Both men and women who have family responsibilities and who are professedly troubled with workaholic tendencies need to face their problem squarely. What are some of the things they must consider in order to bring about a stronger bond between them?

First and foremost is the necessity of giving the spouse the number one place in his or her life. When there is a closeness, nothing will be allowed to crowd in. This includes work. When things are right between husband and wife, the feeling will often sweep over a person's mind, "I just can't wait to get home."

How often do you hear that today? It is not heard because individuals spend little time in sustaining a solid relationship. Couples need to get back to basics, those things that originally attracted each to the other.

One of the problems today is that couples overemphasize

the trivia and fail to accentuate the important things in the marriage. Any marriage counselor will tell you that in nearly all cases, couples who come for counseling complain about the other person. Seldom do they admit to working and maintaining those things inherent in the relationship that drew them to each other in the first place. When these are out of focus there is a greater temptation to stay longer at the office or shop. It becomes a form of escape.

Second, male or female workaholics with family obligations need to take a second look at their respective roles. If those roles are not clearly defined, identity crises may develop whereby a person may feel threatened by the other. Overwork can spell great trouble in a home when one spouse is away a great deal. Those strangled by this dilemma need to determine the work loads at home to alleviate stress.

For example, a working wife who appears to be getting more involved in her job needs empathy and compassion from her husband, not just emotionally but with practicality. He can help to service the home. There is no reason why he cannot assist in the routine shopping or the making of an occasional meal. Why can't he bathe and dress the young children for bed? Men can become very adept at housework with a little effort and loving care and concern for the wife. Who says that roles cannot be switched? Why can't a man push the vacuum? Why can't a husband be useful in the kitchen? After all, most restaurant cooks are men. Why should men be less capable of preparing meals at home?

It seems desirable that wives encourage their husbands to take a more authoritative role in the home. Modern life, in many respects, has forced husbands out of the home situation. This may appear to be a threat to intimacy. It need not. This suggests that the real issue to be worked through is the personal intimacy of the relationship. If the personal bond is firmly set, allowing room for both to function, then the division of authority and labor will logically follow.

The key is for both partners to determine roles even if they may be switched to alleviate work pressure. This should be done by sitting down and talking about it. Just assuming that the other person should or will do something is a mistake. If both agree, there should be no problem.

Third, there must be definite planning for the family in terms of time spent. Each family has the opportunity to set standards that will bring fulfillment for each member. How does a family in today's computerized, impersonal world do that? The answer lies in the desire of those members to plan and build a homelife that has both goals and time built into its schedule.

The survival of the family cannot be left to chance. There are many interruptions and voices vying for the attention of family members. The only way to get around the problem is to set family priorities. People who work extra-long hours on the job need to give special heed. Take those trips, go out for an evening as planned. For that specially planned outing, let nothing except emergency or death disrupt the scheduled event.

Fourth, when a spouse is working excessively, putting strain on the marriage, the partner needs to practice patience and understanding. The less compatible a couple are, the more problems they must resolve. Overwork means that someone is being rejected or shut out. That can be very heavy for the person who feels cut off. More acceptance and love will have to be expressed toward the worker in order to bring greater emotional satisfaction.

As in economics, there is also in marriage a supply-and-demand mechanism at work to maximize productivity in the relationship. With the burdens of overwork, this delicate mechanism must be acknowledged by each spouse and skills of patience must be utilized. Effort in this area can compensate for the corrosion of time spent together.

With concerted effort, the line can be held against the deterioration of a relationship if we remember that we may give without loving, but we cannot truly love without giving. And that means time for the other.

A lack of understanding can bring much frustration in marriage. Often it is difficult to understand where the other person is coming from, because people are complex beings. But

there is a continuing need to try to get closer, through acceptance and loving care, to the person who may have hang-ups
about work habits.

Fifth, the most important ingredient in any marriage is the
building of a personal relationship with God. This will help to
create understanding and will bring the persons closer together. Seeking to please God in the marriage will also help to
sustain commitments made to the partner. And seeking God's
guidance will reaffirm certain personal values which our society has long neglected.

Overwork can be highly destructive of the family. It can
cheat people out of an enriched life. No effort is too great to
combat and overcome its ruinous influences in the family.

6

Around Church, Too— Of All Places!

I feel it is my responsibility; after all, if I don't do it, who will?

BILL Edwards is thirty-eight years old. He has a pretty wife, two beautiful children, and is considered one of the outstanding pastors in his city. Bill and June were married while Bill was still in seminary. Their first child was born during his senior year. June never completed her college education but took a job to help Bill through seminary. Bill is an effective preacher and is greatly respected by both his assistant and the congregation. He works hard on his sermons. His church is growing.

Bill's wife left him at the height of his career. Why? Let's see.

Workaholics are found leading our churches, too! Far more than most of us realize. The problem is that many pastors, without necessarily intending to do so, convey the view by their own work habits, or by preaching, that church work must always have the highest priority. If not, people are often made to feel guilty because they have a split commitment. The message comes through, "Ye cannot serve God and mammon." This obviously is true, but the truth gets garbled through misinterpretation and faulty priorities.

One family was seldom seen in the evening service at church. On several occasions the pastor heard family members being put down indirectly with such remarks as, "My, Bob and

95

Jane, we missed you last Sunday night." Little did people realize that this wise pastor had given counsel to the family. Bob traveled a great deal during the week on his job. As a result he saw very little of his family. One day, feeling guilty, he stopped by the pastor's study. "Pastor, I know I should come to the evening services, but I need to be with my family on Sunday evenings." The pastor wisely advised him to stay home. "Bob," said the minister, "stay home as long as you use the time to be with your family." That minister had rightly seen the issue without creating any guilt for his layman friend.

Clergy Are Not Excluded

Recently a pastor of a large Los Angeles area church was interviewing men for his staff. He asked when they would like to take a day off during the week. He got several different replies: "Oh, it doesn't really matter." "I never take a day off." "I don't really need any time off." The pastor hired none of them.

One day as he interviewed a young prospect, he asked, "What day of the week would you like off?" "Well, I surely don't want Monday off. After the Sunday crunch, I'm in no shape to enjoy the next day. Let me have Thursday off. That's the best day of the week for me." That young man was hired. Wise is he. And, wise is the pastor.

Many ministers work twelve to fifteen hours a day, and some rarely take a day off. There is absolutely nothing meritorious about never having a day or two off each week, or taking holidays to be with your family. Wise is the church board that insists that the pastoral staff take days off and allows them time off for study leaves.

Pastors, when on a holiday, shouldn't preach! They should provide for a change of pace by doing things that are not part of their regular routine. It is extremely important to give the mind and body a chance to regroup and recharge itself. Studies today cite the fact that clergymen occupy one of the most stressful positions in the American labor force.

Unfortunately, one of the tragic illustrations of a workaholic in our modern life is the American pastor. His delusion is that he is married to the church. But let us bring you in on a little secret: the church is already married. That's what the Bible says. In the New Testament the church is pictured as the Bride of Christ.

The minister must, as everyone else, heed the instructions of Scripture. He is in no way exempt from family obligations and responsibilities.

The pastor needs to set his house in order. He needs to set priorities. He often suffers from "fishbowl-itis," the fear of being himself. Because he is immobilized by his own projections, he will frequently live by the whims and fancies of the congregation, always seeking its approval.

Ministers need to heed the Scriptures they so eloquently and expertly expound to others, as for example 1 Timothy 5:8: "But if any provide not for his own, and specially for those of his own house, he hath denied the faith, and is worse than an infidel."

Such a provision indeed may include much more than physical or financial support. If the pastor is overworked, why not reset priorities and share with the congregation the decision to place the family above the church? We believe he will be pleasantly surprised to see a positive response. The people in the pews will accept him more readily for his humanness. They face the same problem. They will appreciate his courage and guidance by example.

A minister a few years ago confessed before his colleagues at a pastors' conference that he was a true workaholic. He did not use the term, but he expressed his addiction to work. He confessed that he was continually informing members of his congregation how hard he worked and the number of hours he was spending in his responsibilities. After being admitted to a local hospital in his Midwest town as a result of complete exhaustion, he had many hours to think about his life and its direction. He came to recognize that he had a felt need to let others know how hard he worked because he believed it was not recognized by his people.

Much that ministers do is never seen. There are no profit-

and-loss columns in the church which point to specific results and, in addition, there are few who dare to be critical of their pastor.

This pastor began to see how he was taken up with trying to prove how worthy and busy he was. Because ledgers and performance charts were never demanded by the church board, he had to prove his productivity in other ways. He realized that a larger budget and increased membership were really the only criteria used to measure his success. As he reflected upon his ministry, he began to see the tyranny under which he was laboring. He had driven himself to a state of exhaustion, feeling all along that he had to be accepted in the eyes of his people.

Ministers are especially vulnerable in this area. Much of their work is unseen and intangible. Somehow, they rationalize, if they put in an overabundance of hours, people will take notice. It is an unhealthy way to look at things and carries with it the inherent danger of having to pay a great price later on.

Church Leaders Get Addicted, Too

Dr. C. Peter Wagner, Associate Professor of Latin American affairs at Fuller Theological Seminary School of World Mission in Pasadena, California, confessed in a published magazine article to being a "converted workaholic." He says that some time ago he had an excruciating headache that lasted for seventy days and sixty-nine nights. He sought spiritual counsel and looked to the Bible for help. He related the following:

> During the ordeal I was under excellent medical treatment. I put myself under the care of a highly competent chiropractor, consulting also with a medical doctor to be sure I was not missing any better option. The chiropractor studied a series of X rays and used a combination of unintelligible polysyllables to describe what was wrong with my muscles, bones and nerves. Three or four visits per

week to his clinic, exercise and diets eventually corrected certain structural defects. But my problem went deeper.[1]

After much soul-searching and spiritual examination, Wagner came to the conclusion that his problem was really very simple. He had been working too hard!

He continued:

> Simple? Who ever heard of God punishing someone for working too hard? I was always taught that work was a virtue. Would God be angry with someone who gave too much to the poor?[2]

Wagner resolved such questions in his mind and came to realize, before it was too late, that there is a price one pays when the addiction to work sets in. He was one of the fortunate ones. Today the term *workaholic* is a daily vocabulary word to him.

Wagner goes on in the article to show how he had fallen into the typical trap of most workaholics, the praise that goes along with hard work. The usual pattern, he confessed, was hearing people comment, "I don't see how you possibly get done all that you do." That, he says, is the supreme pat on the back for the workaholic, and since he craves to hear it as a reward, he will work all the harder to get it. Wagner confessed this pride in productivity.

> Wasn't I proud of propelling myself out of bed and into high gear at 4:30 every morning? Wasn't I proud that while my neighbors were sleeping at 5:00 A.M. (imagine!) I was out in the street running a mile? Wasn't I proud of the number of books and articles I could get published in a year? Wasn't I proud of my ability to bring work home and continue through the evening with only a brief interruption for dinner? Wasn't I proud of foregoing vacations year after year so that I could produce more? Wasn't I proud of the number of miles I could travel and speaking engagements I could handle without a break? Wasn't I proud of dictating fat envelopes of belts on airplanes and shipping them home to my secretary? Wasn't I proud that

when I would land in some exotic country I would invariably choose to work rather than take in the tourist attractions?

Without the headache, I never would have realized what harmful effects this was having on me. I had developed strong guilt feelings about doing anything that would interrupt work. I could not stay in bed more than six hours, would not watch television, could not plan days off or weekends without productive work, and felt uncomfortable when I would go for a drive with the family. I envied some of my friends who could function on only four hours of sleep. But even worse, I found myself judging others for spending their time in such unproductive ways. Imagine, watching the movie on an airplane rather than dictating letters! Through it all, of course, I easily rationalized it as "serving God," a simple process for a clergyman, but handy also for almost any Christian workaholic.[3]

From the Pulpit to the Pew

Not only do we recognize the fact that there are workaholics in the pulpit, but we have workaholics by the score who sit in church pews. The payoff here, contrary to popular saintly conviction, is not necessarily future crowns but present crises.

One of the great problems facing any Christian church is in the area of volunteerism. The church is one of the most unique functioning institutions in the world. It has few people on the payroll and it depends almost entirely upon volunteers. It is remarkable that it gets along as well as it does.

But volunteerism can be another beautiful form of escape. It is the cloak or mantle. It may be the most severe form of the workaholic disease, because it gives the appearance of godly dedication and "do-goodism." Clergy, as we've stated, head the list.

The way to join the workaholic clique at church is to stop most family responsibilities. Forget family functions, ignore your spouse's things-to-do-at-home list, forget all school functions, and let the house fall into disrepair. By all means, quit socializing with friends.

Now the decks are cleared. You can begin volunteering. And, you know what? It is amazing how many people will move over and let you roll up your sleeves. Now, we don't want to discredit volunteering. Without it the church could scarcely exist in any form.

But if you get the disease, better—or should we say worse— things may lurk ahead. You'll get plenty of praise and—for a time—your family won't dare criticize.

Consider what Bill Little says in his charming and captivating book:

> Volunteers are in demand everywhere. Branch out. Start with jobs that really need doing, and then leap into any group that gives you a badge, button, banner, chair to sit in, place to stand, letter to write, phone to dial or answer, literature to hand out, beads to count, toothpaste to test, cheese to taste, birds to inventory, leaves to collect or wild animals to round up for the ark. Strangers will admire and love you, while your problems snowball and your real responsibilities pile up like an avalanche of manure on your family and friends.
>
> You may someday be crowned Volunteer of the Year. Such an honor will enable you to feel total rejection and misunderstanding from unappreciative children and friends, who during your absence have been compelled to assume your legitimate responsibilities. You are now a prime candidate for depression because you have no one with whom to share your hour of glory. They have all departed to other mates, step-parents or friends or may be convalescing in a rest home. Now you not only have problems; you are a genuine problem and are ready for VA [Volunteerics Anonymous].[4]

These well-stated thoughts have a strong application around the church grounds.

The problem of heavy, unbalanced involvement in church affairs is a major one in church circles. For the Christian worker, there oftentimes is tremendous frustration in the fact that people feel impelled and compelled to work in, around, and through the church. If we don't "carry our full fair load" we feel like we are cheating God and the church. Far too often we are guilty of doing "church work" rather than "the work of the church."

Like regimented sheep, some people will be out to trustees' meeting on Monday, prayer meeting on Wednesday, choir practice on Thursday, half a day on Saturday with a hammer and saw on work day, and then will spend nearly all day Sunday at church or Sunday school and two church services. And, all in the name of Christian service.

Far too many who are afflicted with the problem of overwork at church seek to work out their Christian frustrations by taking on extra and added assignments. They need to learn the necessity of being able to say no.

But what makes it so tough is the universal temptation to glorify work in the church. The rationalizations are rampant: "He may have family problems, but look what he's doing for the Lord and the church!"

Church people are taught to decry idolatry in any form. They can quote the Ten Commandments on this subject. But the irony is that many of them make religious work an idolatry in itself, at the expense of other important areas of life.

Workaholics at church range from the pastor, the bishop, the secretary, the janitor, and the overly-conscientious parishioner. You may be dubbed a fanatic, but they're right, a fanatic for work. "The place can't get along without me. Look at my zeal, my dedication."

A friend of a minister was talking to him in the church office. The door was open. Across the entrance walked a woman in her late thirties. "See that woman?" asked the pastor. "She practically lives here." He once suggested she put a bed up someplace, but she wouldn't take the hint. "She does everything around here, and she's got a family."

Doesn't the Lord say that our prime responsibility is to our families? What's her problem? It could be a number of things. Perhaps she's so loaded with guilt that it's her way to atone. It might be that she has such a poor self-image that she needs the

Lord's and others' approval. Maybe she's trying to escape from the responsibilities at home. She might have a delusional system that makes her feel extra-important, indispensable. We'd like to think it is sheer dedication. More often it is not. She may not realize it at all, but she's trying to compensate for something in her life by working excessively around the church.

A beautiful young lady, but depressed and very uptight. That was the pastor's assessment.

The church workaholic doesn't know it, but he's probably playing god a little, while within himself he can't discern what's really right or wrong in a given situation. Even "too much church" can turn out to be a sour note in one's life.

Many church workaholics need much approval. As we've suggested, this is often done under the guise of service. How often we use the term "serving the Lord." This convenient label can be used to feed one's approval needs which in the end is not pleasing to God at all, because other important areas of life may be wanting or barren.

The church workaholic would rather say yes than be rejected by some other church member who might think he was not very committed or dedicated to God. He becomes *promise laden* because he so desperately needs to be seen as *spiritual* to gain acceptance.

Check out your motives. You may have a nagging conscience. You haven't a moment's peace. That's not a very good motive for working in the church. You never will have peace unless you deal with the guilt and throw off the burden of approval needs.

I Thought the Lord Couldn't Get Along Without Me

The following article in a popular Christian magazine sets forth the problems that many people in the church face.

I have been a workaholic for the Lord.

Don't think I'm boasting or complaining. The problem is that my concept of "the Lord's work" and what He expects has been distorted. I have wrong priorities.

I wasn't spending enough time with my family, but I excused myself. "After all, it's the Lord's work." Sometimes, I'm ashamed to admit, I subconsciously thought that the Lord's work couldn't get along without me.

Recently, [something] occurred that [has] made me reassess my involvement in church work.

One evening my son Jon was having trouble with his school work. He came to me while I was busy poring over some church reports. "Dad," he asked, "can you help me with this problem?"

"Can't you see I'm busy?" I snapped.

The expression on his face as he started back to his room made me try to make it right. "Just a minute. I'll see if I can help."

He looked at me and said, "Never mind. I'll get it. You're too busy again." I could see a wall building between us that would grow more impenetrable each time I was "too busy."

Soon I became convinced that I had become a workaholic. All the things I had been doing were for worthy causes. But I am convinced that not all of them were "the Lord's work," at least not for me.[5]

How many Christian workaholics are there? Probably far more than any of us ever realize. They are suffering more than they themselves realize. Their families are suffering. They don't have many friends. Few people reach out to help them.

The church should be in the forefront to help such people and it should be more critically aware of what is taking place right on its front steps. Church people are no more immune than nonchurch folk. Overwork in a church can cause headaches, marital problems, and heart attacks just like any other place.

What Is Meant by Success?

Perhaps the basic problem for church people is to assess what they mean by success. Many find themselves so absorbed in church work they lose sight of other facets of their lives which are also highly important. Workaholics in the church somehow get caught up in the secular world's concepts of success, which are primarily based upon performance. This naturally puts a tremendous amount of pressure upon the individual in terms of time invested in church work.

Dr. Vernon C. Grounds, president of the Conservative Baptist Theological Seminary in Denver, Colorado, was the 1977 Gordon College (Wenham, Massachusetts) commencement speaker. In that address he spoke about worldly standards and how Christians often confuse the real meaning of success. He stated: "Worldly success is one thing; spiritual success is totally different. Worldly success is success judged without preference to God or eternity. Spiritual success is success as judged by God, success from the perspective of eternity, success without reference to the world's evaluation."

Success in the world, he added, is determined by public impact and it is "judged entirely by superiority in beauty (Liz Taylor), brawn (Joe Namath), or brains (Albert Einstein) . . . . The person with a higher status in society is the superior person."

Unknowingly the church today has borrowed this definition from the secularist. "To be successful you have to compete for the sake of competing, win for the sake of winning. And, the one who gets the honors is the one who does it all without pause or letup—the fastest, the sportiest, the artiest."

This dynamic operates in much of Christian service—the desire to be noticeably superior, first if possible, number one; never number two.

Dr. Grounds makes the further application: "The church has allowed the world to impose on Christian service standards of success which are utterly nonbiblical; and when I talk of the church in this context I mean American evangelicalism . . . . As disciples of Jesus Christ, too many of us are sinfully concerned about size—the size of sanctuaries, the size of salaries, the size of Sunday schools. Too many of us are sinfully preoccupied with statistics about budgets and buildings and buses and baptism."

Such an overemphasis can drive men and women in churches to overwork, all in the name of "Christian service."

Indeed, timely words for all related to the church to hear.

Where Is Your Wife?

We are addressing ourselves here as today's leaders, and especially as married men. Where does your wife fit in with your priorities? Certainly, of all the human relationships described in the Bible, the highest and most significant is the one found in marriage. The Apostle Paul could only compare it to the relationship of Christ and His church (Ephesians 5:21–33).

The disruption of this relationship can have tremendous spiritual consequences. Peter tells us that interruption of the relationship can even interfere with our prayers (1 Peter 3:7).

Is your ministry as a leader built upon a foundation of a strong marriage relationship, or does it move forward in spite of that relationship?

What About Your Calling?

Some of us may immediately respond in our own defense, "But this is the work to which God has called me! My wife understands that. That's one of the sacrifices that we are making together."

Perhaps. But perhaps that is *your* view of the situation, and although it may be outwardly shared by your wife, inwardly (consciously or unconsciously) she may feel quite differently.

Too often the wife is put in the position of appearing to oppose the work if she does not feel at ease with the circumstances within which her husband is moving. Many men and women marry before they have a clear picture of the ministry to which they (or he) may be called. Too often a man may overlook what God may be saying to his wife and what gifts He has bestowed upon her. Many men will often just run roughshod over their wives' views or judgments.

It's an Uphill Battle

The wife of a dynamic pastor or Christian leader may be in an uphill battle for survival as a person. Many times she has sacrificed herself and her own education only to see her husband become educated right out of her intellectual life. The public affirmation that comes to him and the sense of accomplishment that he feels in pursuing his career, can only be shared by her in a secondhand way.

Of course, there are many husband/wife teams who really *are* teams. They truly have had a common call to the work for which the husband may be employed. They see themselves as sharing a joint ministry. But for many this is far from the case. And, as the initial intensive occupation with raising a family and becoming established is exchanged for the changing realities of mid-life, many wives of executives—Christian and otherwise—begin to wonder whether this is all there is to living. Many conclude that it is not.

If you are having a problem in your home, prayerfully consider whether you really do believe that your priorities are valid. Remember, they are cited in the Bible. God's work *will* get done without you! God is really not nervous about the future. Isn't He much more concerned with what you *are* than what you accomplish, and isn't what you are demonstrated by the relationships that you have? And isn't the most profound of those relationships the one that you have with your wife?

Have you left your wife?

We pray she will take you back.

Where are you as a Christian leader or layman? Where does your commitment lie? Could it be that you, too, are one of those, perhaps without even knowing it, who has left his wife?

How do you sort it all out? Where do your Christian priorities lie? How does one find a balance between commitment to the task and commitment to one's family?

It all basically comes down to a matter of priorities. More than one family has been lost to a father or mother because the parent simply felt that the work he or she was *called* to do within the church was more important than relating to the family.

Wives, these words are for you, too. Are you neglecting your husband and your family by overworking at the church?

It is well to remember to get your priorities straightened out, or clarified:

- God first
- Family second
- Fellow Christians third
- Work of Christ fourth.

All are extremely important, but if they get out of order or off balance, you may have to start looking for a new family.

Part II

The Causes Regulating the Work Trap

7

The Workaholic:
A Product of His Culture

*In our firm we really do want and
need a few workaholics around to
keep the place going and growing.*

SOME time ago a photo appeared in a major city newspaper in which an executive was seen receiving a year-end award for excellence in performance. The caption extolled this man for his dedication to his work. It further stated, "And Harry has not taken a vacation in three years!" Left out was the fact that he had a wife and three children. We wonder how they felt about the award!

The covering story stated that Harry was asked to comment upon his achievement. His only reply: "Hard work never hurt anybody."

Many of the forces that drive men and women toward achievement emanate from what we call our "American way of life." You have listened to commencement speakers, in high school or college. "Aim high," they challenge. "Hitch your wagon to a star." Youths are exhorted to grow up to be corporation presidents or to strive for recognition and prestige. In our hero worship we look to the self-made man, the rags-to-riches, log-cabin-to-the-White-House or from-the-Little-League-to-the-Big-League type of person for our success stories.

Perhaps we would do better to challenge our youth to aim low! It would possibly be more helpful to suggest that they attain more achievable goals, and then proceed to the next higher level. This may prevent the person from crashing down in failure. There would be far less disillusionment, disappointment, and despair if work and careers could be approached in a more realistic manner.

There is no question that one of the basic contributors to our present growing problem of workaholism is the influence of our present culture. Our friend Harry, without even realizing it, was no doubt a product of cultural conditioning. Somewhere, someplace, out of his past he received a message that work, hard work if you please, is the primary or highest experience of man and that vacation or leisure time is a waste and even, at times, shameful. Perhaps this was the philosophy of his father or grandfather. He may have picked it up from his colleagues at work. In any event, Harry is a victim of cultural conditioning.

What do we mean by culture?

For the purposes of definition, for us in this book, culture means "the total way of life of a people, the modes of behavior and thought which become cumulative and are transmitted from generation to generation."[1] John Miner says further that the crucial determinants, when one views performance within a society, are the cultural values. These he interprets to be the concepts of right and wrong which, in turn, constitute the ethical systems and moral precepts of right and wrong, which then become the ideals of the society.[2] To better understand our culture and our American work ethic, let us examine a few historical facts.

Transferred Values

The work ethic seems to have had its beginnings with Martin Luther, the father of the Reformation. This historical ethic was one of the roots of the American economy. Luther sought to endow the idea of work with a religious dignity by calling attention to the fact that it is a holy calling. He believed, as did later Reformers, that by engaging in work a person was serving God, regardless of the rewards. John Calvin saw work not only as a religious duty:

. . . but men were called upon to work without desire for the fruit of their labor simply because to work is the will of God. Such work would establish God's kingdom on earth, and this was its value and its end.[3]

David Macarov states that this attitude toward work was brought to this country by the Puritans who also perceived work and the acquisition of money as an end in itself. It was an ascetic discipline.[4] He indicates that inherent within the Protestant ethic was the view that man *should* want to work hard and get ahead. He *should* want to make money.

Macarov states that the Protestant ethic was the force behind the industrialization of the cities in this country, and eventually for the whole nation. He says that when and where the ethic was strong there was a religious belief in the efficacy of work for attaining salvation or the blessings of God.

A popular writer, poking fun at the Puritan work ethic, said that it means "If it doesn't hurt . . . it's no good."

Other ideas within the ethic may have been weak because they were based upon a false interpretation of life.

One reason it is so difficult to deal with the problem of workaholism is that society reinforces it rather than condemns it. After all, we say, it was essentially the hard worker who built this country to greatness. That's why it's difficult to knock him. He's conscientious—we owe a debt of gratitude to him. The misinterpretation of this Protestant ethic makes the hard worker the paradigm of virtue. Bible proof texts are easy to come by if one wants to stretch a point for justification, as some of our Puritan ancestors have done.

Regardless of what one may think about the work ethic, there was much good in it because it set the tone for economic growth unmatched in world history. In addition, it helped man to see the spiritual nature of his secular vocations.

One thing perhaps needs to be made clear at this point. Protestants do not have any special claim on the term *work ethic*. For the sake of discussion, we retain the term because of its familiarity and common usage. But all responsible people affirm most of its basic truths. It might better be termed the

Judeo-Christian ethic because it has a sound biblical base in both the Old and New Testaments.

Power and the drive to get ahead are fundamental needs for most people. We need the satisfaction that comes from the feelings of independence and autonomy. These drives are as truly American as baseball, apple pie, and hot dogs. They were an integral part of the founding of our nation. We are proud of the early revolutionaries. We idealize the pioneer and the entrepreneur. We glorify them to our children because we want them, as well, to be strong, assertive, and independent.

Many workaholics cannot tolerate inactivity or dependency. They must be constantly at work, exerting energy. "After all, our forefathers worked hard. Look where it got us." These ideas are lifted right out of the Protestant ethic—distorted, to some degree. The cultural conditioning, over the centuries, has left its mark upon us today.

Wayne Oates summarizes the Protestant work ethic well when he says:

> A universal taboo is placed on *idleness*, and *industri-ousness* is considered a religious ideal; *waste* is a vice, and *frugality* a virtue; complacency and failure are out-lawed, and *ambition* and *success* are taken as sure signs of God's favor; the universal sign of sin is *poverty*, and the crowning sign of God's favor is *wealth*.[5]

Oates goes on to make the point that the workaholic, even without knowing it, has embraced this ethic as his personal religion. It reflects the ethic of industriousness, frugality, ambition, and success as primary virtues. In and of themselves, they are good but the workaholic becomes idolatrous with respect to them.

Regardless of the influences of the Protestant ethic, whether pro or con, there is no question that a work ethic is absolutely essential for life-fulfilling needs. There may be negative elements inherent in the Puritan ideals brought to this country, but their views may be conceived as a misinterpretation of truth when determining the disciplines of life.

We must not throw out the baby with the bath water! Basic

absolutes must be retained in order to preserve a society. The business world is no exception.

Peter F. Drucker was one of the first scientific observers of American industry at the end of World War II to take note of trends in business and labor. He sees the need for an ethic:

> In the pursuit of its everyday private practice and in performing its economic job, big business is therefore expected to further human values and to serve national purpose. This, rather than matters of ordinary honesty or fastidiousness (e.g., kick-back or call-girl problems discussed so ponderously today), is at the core of big-business ethics.[6]

We can move away from some negative carry-overs of the old work ethic if we remember that the need for a satisfying work ethic does not have to be reduced simply to *shalt not*'s. Rather, it is positive, too, as noted when we discussed the biblical concepts earlier.

Translated Into Modern Life

There is no question that our present-day culture contributes greatly to workaholism. In our highly competitive society the technical atmosphere is extremely demanding and overpowering. The dynamic forces of publicity and the division of labor which becomes so impersonal cause workers to seek ways to compensate or to work through their frustrations. Such a problem may arouse aggressive tendencies which may lead to outbursts of anger and the need for acting out the internal conflicts.

We recognize that the crunch at work is leading Americans more and more to escape after work. The lure, too, is of "being one's own boss." Many try it. Thousands of small businesses fail. The crunch leads many to boredom, absentmindedness, accident-proneness, and a myriad of obsessive reveries.

Lack of Value

One thing we must become aware of is that our culture does spawn addictive behavior, whether it be alcohol, drugs, or overwork. There are reasons why a cancer eats away at our society. William H. Whyte makes some very telling points in his excellent book *The Organization Man* in which he says that the organization man or woman lacks certain values as a human being. Individuals in our modern world of commerce are submerged in and to the omnipotence of the firm. They are subordinated for the "good of the company." They must protect and build up the firm. Never mind personhood—the company comes first.

The individual must always be on call, as well, for the company. The most telling description, according to Whyte, is that the person "is so involved in his work he cannot distinguish between work and the rest of his life—and he is happy that he cannot." [7]

Distorted Standards

We live in a culture that is counterproductive in many ways. The mores and standards imposed upon us often work against our becoming whole, mature persons. These standards often obscure reality and produce a confused state. Our culture produces many double binds in which we are damned if we do and damned if we don't.

One of these widely held standards is the overvaluation we place upon work. This is a spin-off of the deeper societal emphasis upon performance as a measure of success. We have somehow developed the notion that the person who stays late at the office or goes in to work on the weekend is a most dedicated fellow. His performance demonstrates his work loyalty. Our notion is that he is really a company man and will be certain to be the one in line for the next promotion.

To add to the confusion, the workaholic is further duped into thinking that he is indispensable. He's a vital cog. He's loaded with all kinds of boastful fantasies: "They'll never make it without me"; "No one can make the sale like I can"; "If I don't do it, who will or can?"

The addiction sets in when one really believes these kinds of statements.

In addition, there are workaholic companies that thrust

work upon people. They expect people to respond to their continual beck and call. One employer was known to have consistently called his staff into his office ten minutes before quitting time and planned for long conferences. He admitted later that he wanted to get "as much out of his people as possible." He indicated that it made up for all the cigarette-and-coffee breaks and the little conversations about personal matters. Some companies even encourage the skipping of lunch for the sake of urgent business. And how many insist on making lunches "working lunches"!

Somehow, work addicts seem to wind up in such places. When being interviewed for a new position, it is wise to ask how management perceives the role of the family in an employee's life. It does not take long to get an accurate reading about a boss's or firm's philosophy of work and the level of expectation about work.

Like work addicts themselves, such organizations lack imagination. They reflect the personal views and emotional hangups of their leaders.

Overdone *Should*'s

We live in a world of *should*'s. The psychologist says this is necessary to structure a superego. However, there are vast gray areas in life where individuals may practice freedom and decide on their own growth pace.

Our culture has done us much disservice. "You should make money." "You should get to the top." "You should get ahead." For some, that may be fine if they are able to balance such *should*'s with satisfying relationships. You may want to make a lot of money. Fine. But you must just as urgently consider time with your family, time for leisure, time for avocation, and a realistic schedule which includes adequate rest.

These *should*'s are clearly manifested in no better way than the means we use to thrust our youth into the world, often before they reach maturity. "You're big enough and old enough now, son, to go out and support yourself." Being suddenly expected to assume his own economic responsibilities with a "when I was your age, I . . . " kind of lecture may place before a person an impossible or very frightening standard which he will be unable to handle later on.

Misguided Views on Success

Another discredit our current culture has done for the American worker is to mislead him in terms of success. Today's workaholic labors under some false notions about what success is.

Dr. Eugene Jennings has done extensive research into the meaning of success for today's executives. He believes that many define it in terms of mobility. Success is moving up toward the top, while failure is being passed over. "Success is mobility. It is not so much position, title, salary, or exceptional performance as it is success in moving and movement." [8]

Success, then, in our culture, is the drive to achieve based on the *ability to perform* in order to move up the ladder. Earlier in our nation's history a man would be content with doing a job well. To him, that was success. Today, success for many means being advanced, promoted. Movement then is a means to an end.

That may mean having no lasting satisfaction and little contentment. The scramble toward the top makes for dissatisfaction, rivalry, and hard feelings in many cases. One executive in an Eastern firm, when hiring a new man, would say, "If you're not interested in taking my job away from me, you're not the kind of man I want around here."

Many won't care if a promotion is not offered; they will be satisfied. For the workaholic that would represent failure, a personal disaster. It would destroy his self-confidence and perhaps create an identity crisis.

Closely related is the value many workaholics place upon money as a measure of success. Money reassures. It provides status, and thus builds the ego. A man may not be certain about his social status, but he knows how much money he makes.

One interesting phenomenon of our time—beyond the

simplistic claim that our American culture, and more specifically our business community, fosters workaholism—is that the very professionals who are called in to treat and counsel workaholics are often themselves addicts to work. They appear to suffer from the same symptoms—lack of sleep, poor diet, hypertension, and being totally and exclusively committed to their work.

Many doctors, for example, don't know what to do for the problem, for many themselves overwork. They do not practice exercise and relaxation and, therefore, they don't prescribe it. They are much too ready to prescribe some chemical answer in the form of antidepressant medication which in itself may lead to another addiction.

Our society and culture is rightfully concerned with drug and alcohol addicts. Large federal and state institutions have been created for their care and treatment. These are rightly seen by our culture as serious problems. Unfortunately, there is quite a different attitude toward workaholism. It would appear that society actually lauds and praises a person in the labor market who is driven to excessive work. Many firms expect it. The only thing, seemingly, that counts is business growth. Forget the individual. "What he does outside of work is his business," is the flippant attitude of too many.

At one of our management seminars a top-level businessman was overheard to say, "In our firm we really do want and need a few workaholics around to keep the place going and growing." How sad!

8

Getting Caught in the Work Trap

*A man is not a failure if he makes a
mistake; it's only failure when he
starts blaming something else for it.*

"THE devil made me do it," comedian Flip Wilson would say.
That was his standard response when he would be caught in
some sort of trouble. The causes of human behavior are multiple, and Flip had his answer. The reasons why people get
caught in the work trap are likewise numerous. Let's look at
some of them.

On the surface it appears that the real motivation for excessive work is so often the need for more money. Thus, the need
to stay at the office longer or bring the work home, or the need
to get that extra job. However, beneath the surface lie other
very subtle factors that should be viewed to more fully understand the problem.

These factors make for some nice little rationalizations. "I
surely don't want my wife to have to work." "I want the kids to
have it easier than I had it." "I have to make sure my kids get a
college education." "Of course, our family needs two cars. My
wife can't stay stuck at home all the time, there are too many
errands to be run." They all sound so good, but the vise gets
noticeably tighter and tighter.

What many people do not realize is that a great deal of what
we do or think comes from unconscious associations with our
past. Emotional problems often exist because people were

deprived of or thwarted from having close, loving relationships.

To remain mentally healthy, one has to give vent to the disturbing influences of his existence. Every day our bodies cleanse themselves of harmful toxins through processes of waste eliminations. If these toxins were allowed to accumulate, they would cause us to sicken and would eventually kill us.

Our minds, too, become filled with toxins—the disturbing residue of assorted hurts, worries, fears, and traumas. Tucked away in the corners and recesses of our subconscious, they may surface to bother us occasionally, but their toxic influence is usually minimal, causing, at most, vague anxieties and now-and-then sadness.

But at other times these mental toxins build up to the point where they become disruptive to our emotional and psychological functioning. Symptoms of this psychological *poisoning* can show up as severe stress, nervousness, anxiety, and stress-related physical problems such as colitis, migraines, and tinnitus (ear noise) or, more seriously, as deep depression and even psychosis.

Take the true experience of Glen. He was so busy working continuously that he had no close friends. He was so bound to his desk at work that management failed to take him into their confidence because they hardly knew him. He deeply desired recognition, but never allowed his resentful feelings to surface.

Later his company shifted him to a new job. Intellectually he approved, but he was angry because he was not consulted prior to the decision. He interpreted this to mean that he was not appreciated. He supported the view by reminding himself that he had received only minimal salary increases for several years.

Later, he came to learn that he was a victim of his own silence because management assumed that he was satisfied with his role. His overwork actually militated against him because he gave little of himself emotionally to others.

His feelings of not being appreciated had their roots in his childhood. He had had a stormy upbringing. He learned to sublimate his feelings in more positive areas. This worked for a time, but ultimately his bitterness became too strong and the protective barrier began to break down. Emergency defenses were set in motion: depression, self-depreciation, and psychosomatic illnesses.

We've all read success stories of how hard work brought men to great wealth, power, and prestige. But shortly after they reached the pinnacle, they collapsed—physically or mentally. Others work hard, not for economic reasons, but for purely psychological needs.

There is little question that many workaholics use their work as a defense against some form of anxiety, either from without or from within. Anxiety is both a painful experience and a warning of impending danger. This forces a person to do something about it. Either the person will cope and deal with the anxiety, or his ego will resort to some irrational protective measure known as a *defense mechanism.*

To defend itself, the ego will respond to trauma, conflict, or hurt either by attacking, withdrawing, compromising, or accommodating it. One psychologist says that the ego will either be put to *fight* or *flight.* We all use defenses to sustain our identity. The problem comes when they are used in unhealthy ways to avoid conflict which should be dealt with. What we don't realize is that these mechanisms usually operate on the unconscious level and they become habitual. Therefore they may lead to a measure of self-deception and reality distortion. We too often do not realistically cope with a stressful situation.

To understand better what is meant by defense mechanism, consider the complaint by a wife who, whenever her husband lost an article, would ask, "Why did you lose it?" or "Where did you lose it, dear?" He would invariably reply, "I didn't lose it; it just disappeared." Rather amusing, but how sad. Here is a man who is unable to handle criticism or to admit wrong. His way of dealing with the issue is to deny that he had any part in the problem. The lost article in question just suddenly picked up and took off! And, it got to the point where, by a trick of the mind, he began to at least half believe it.

Everyone tries to deal with anxiety on the basis of how he has learned to cope, usually very early in childhood. It is then we begin to learn how to rationalize our behavior. That becomes reality even though to others it may seem to be irrational. Reality is therefore not the same for everyone. It is easy to forget that different people see things in different ways.

How often do you see a person do something that appears to you to be a stupid form of behavior? "How could they do such a dumb thing?" we ask ourselves. "Facts are facts." But we must remember that people deal with facts from the background of their own experience and perception.

That's why the alcoholic drinks. Drinking works for him; it kills emotional pain. "Better living through chemistry," is his motto. Let's not forget that the work addict has his own framework of reality and people respond to him according to their own perceptions.

That is why we must be sensitive to the workaholic. He is living in what to him is reality. It may be highly destructive, but he has reasoned it out for himself. We must, then, be careful to be as nonjudgmental as possible. Sensitivity and caring love must be communicated to such a person who has deliberately chosen, whether on a conscious or unconscious level, to use work as a means of cutting himself off from others.

One may manipulate someone to get the affection he thinks he needs, drink excessively to drown sorrow or stress, or act like a bully when he feels inferior. These actions have the same general effect: they make us less aware of the pain.

Because conflict can promote such defensive actions as drinking, boasting, or working harder, it reveals that everyone has some anxieties and some defenses. Some, however, are more destructive than others.

The world approves and rewards men who sacrifice to get ahead but generally disapproves of drinking and boasting as acceptable behavior. The braggart and the hard-charger may have the same psychological problems (feelings of inadequacy) but very different objective problems. The braggart alienates people, harms his career, and feels even more inadequate, whereas the hard-charger gains respect, advances his career, and may feel more adequate.

The amount of anxiety a man feels may therefore be less important than the way he handles it. Defenses are a part of everyone's "psychic economy." They control anxiety and keep this economy functioning. Sometimes they are too costly and don't provide very good protection against anxiety; they may create other problems or fail to preserve comfort.[1]

Defenses, therefore, contribute to one's well-being by letting one express his feelings in less costly ways.

As stated, certain defenses are useful because they can help a person attain economic and other kinds of success. Many individuals have used defenses to achieve, when deep within themselves they felt inferior or inadequate. Even though there may be some cost in sacrificing social relationships, an obsession with money and profit can drive a person to control his anxiety over having been reared in a ghetto or in an impoverished home.

But, as Alan Schoonmaker points out, defenses can be "self-defeating because they can work only if a person deceives himself, and self-deception becomes more difficult and exhausting as time goes on."[2]

When it comes to work, the true workaholic uses it as a rebuttal to the trauma or psychic pain experienced earlier in life. But the harnessing of aggressive energy in work can break down and create untold havoc. We recognize these defense mechanisms as symptoms of illness. The greater illness awaits ahead—the inability to work and the inability to control the excess of hostility—which is behind the whole pattern.

Consider some of the basic defenses the workaholic may use in order to deal with some aspects of his or her life.

Repression.   By definition, *repression* is the active process of keeping out, ejecting, and banishing from consciousness ideas or impulses that are unacceptable to it. It is quite simply an avoidance technique. The unfortunate thing about it is that it prevents a person from discovering who he really is, because it blocks feelings and pushes them out of his focus of awareness.

A good illustration of repression might be an individual who has suffered through a natural catastrophe, such as a flood or an earthquake. He goes to a first-aid station but remembers nothing about what happened. Repression is not a simple psychic function. One psychiatrist says that it is more than just forgetting something. It is forgetting that we have forgotten.[3]

Repression is probably the defense most used by workaholics. It helps to keep unpleasant memories and feelings out of consciousness. We try to forget the grief over the loss of a loved one. A woman forgets the intense pain of childbirth. When recalling experiences of the past, we tend to remember only the happy memories and forget the unpleasantries.

Repression is often more than forgetting. We repress the things we consider to be unpleasant or avoid the things we consider unimportant.

Usually we do not consciously choose to repress. We do it automatically in those areas where we may be hurt by someone or some stimulus in our environment. At this point, a distinction should be made between forgetting and repressing:

> . . . repression is much more complete and permanent. If we forget something, we can easily be reminded of it. A service station, a radio commercial, or an oil truck can remind us to buy gasoline. Thinking about dinner or our children can remind us to buy a quart of milk. When something is repressed, reminders usually do not work. We resist being reminded of our repressed feelings or memories even if they are obvious to other people.[4]

Repression as a defense may help us in time to overcome anxiety and to live with ourselves, but sometimes it is not strong enough to completely protect us. We may, for example, push down deep hatred for a person, but will express that intense feeling indirectly, in overly criticizing him. We may repress our strong hate for authority figures, but get sadistic joy out of watching a boxer get pummeled into a knockout in the seventh round.

One thing we should know about repression is that it can become a means of blocking all feelings. A person who consistently blocks negative or bad feelings, such as anger and fear, will also automatically block good feelings as well.

One workaholic admitted while in therapy, "I need to work constantly because I just lose myself in my job. I'd go crazy if I couldn't work all the time. It's great to be able to forget my troubles."

Many workaholics use overwork to eliminate threatening thoughts, beliefs, and memories by blocking awareness of what's going on around them. It is their way of helping to reduce anxiety.

We should realize that when feelings are repressed they do not go out of existence. Science has told us for years that matter cannot be destroyed, it just changes form. We now know that neither can energy be destroyed. It must go someplace. Repressed material does not die within. It remains in our mind and often will come back to haunt us with tremendous force. For example, unexpressed anger may later lead to severe depression and then psychosomatic conditions. It may also lead to morbid thoughts and bizarre behavior.

Work used as a repressive defense measure conceals the true factors that direct a person's behavior. The likely result is that he will choose misguided goals. Because they turn out in the long run to be dissatisfying, such choices may lead to failure and feelings of self-contempt and the use of other destructive defense mechanisms.

Isolation. Escape is one of the major defenses of the isolated workaholic. He would rather stay on the job than go home. A college student related an experience which occurred during his school days. He had gone home with a friend for a weekend. When they arrived near his buddy's home, they drove past his father's place of business before going to his house. His friend predicted a hundred miles before their arrival, "I bet my ol' man will still be working when we pull in."

Sure enough. It was 11:00 P.M. The light in his office was still on. The friend reported with disappointment that it was not uncommon for his father to sleep at his place of work.

A number of reasons may exist for such an escape. It may be the dread of facing conflict in close relationships, a difficult marriage, or the fact that work is more pleasurable than what happens at home.

One man, in being counseled, confessed that he liked the people on the job more than those in his own family. He thus chose isolation, staying at his work as much as he could. Psychology teaches us that there are people who possess *schizoid* tendencies in their personality. This term must be differentiated from schizophrenia, which is a form of psychosis. The workaholic who uses work to isolate himself for whatever reason may use this as a defense against anxiety.

Workaholics who are schizoid, without question use work as an escape mechanism to avoid close personal relationships. The symptoms of their emotional problems are detachment, aloofness, and noninvolvement. At times they can get involved, but they would rather not. When they do, they have little interest because they are cut off, out of touch. Since they are so preoccupied with themselves, this leaves them oblivious to other people's feelings. Their tendency is not to hear quiet expressions or low-key criticisms. They just are not in tune with others on a feeling level.

The loner workaholic, being isolated, uses other various psychological defenses which make it safer for him to deny the real world of people. He enjoys his fantasy world because he does not have to face confrontation. Worse still, in such retreat he seldom sees how other people react to his behavior.

This is most unfortunate because we grow emotionally by getting feedback from others. The isolated workaholic is immature because his noninvolvement with people blocks growth. He can't stand losing an argument because it upsets the safe, fantasy world he has created. Anxiety is created because it is impossible for him to totally shut people out. They are always a threat to him. He has not learned to deal with them. This means that he has difficulty working or playing with them for any length of time, because of the fear that they will manipulate him to their own advantage, just as his parents did.

This kind of approach to the real world means loss of contact. The possibility of keeping or gaining friends is remote because the loner drives them away.

Workaholics who use work as an escape inhibit themselves from expressing anger through repressed isolation. They will often, therefore, express an overabundance of kindness, not wanting to create waves. They will attempt to avoid confrontation and arguments. They need constant reassurance that everything is moving along satisfactorily.

The isolated workaholic cannot be forced into a prescribed mold. There are varying gradations of the problem, depending upon the extent or the depth of the neurosis. All of them, however, appear to answer narcissistic hurts with simple denials and a protective covering. The person who is more severely disturbed emotionally may tend to react to frustrations with the loss of objective relationships.

One of the characteristics noted in schizoid persons is that, lacking contact with people, they become void of emotional expressions and generally appear to be emotionally inadequate.

> Frequently, emotions are entirely lacking in situations where they are to be expected. A lack of emotions which is due not to mere repressions but to real loss of contact with the objective world gives the observer a specific impression of "queerness." [5]

The workaholic as an isolate has a decided deficiency in spontaneity. Martin Haskell, in his excellent work which he considers an alternative to psychoanalysis, defines spontaneity as "the variable degree of adequate response to a situation with a variable degree of novelty." [6] In other words, the spontaneous person is able to respond by bringing into a given situation appropriate roles. However, indifference, apathy, coldness, and isolation toward people are certainly symptoms indicating varying degrees of deficiency in spontaneity. Haskell states:

The more spontaneous a man is the better is he able to deal effectively with problems arising in the course of any of his relationships, personal or societal. He demonstrates an increased awareness of the many alternatives available to him. This awareness of alternatives makes him free to choose and free to act. Increased spontaneity enables man to improve his relationships with his wife or move to an alternative solution of his marital problems. He is also better able to derive satisfactions in his occupation or choose another.[7]

Rationalization. Another common defense used by the workaholic is to accept superficially plausible explanations to justify his behavior or feelings that may be believed to be wrong. This can be illustrated in many ways. Take for example the fox, in Aesop's Fable, which was unable to reach the grapes. It rationalized that they were perhaps sour anyway. Then consider the politician who justifies his shady political deals by rationalizing that it would be unfortunate for society to elect his opponent. Or, people who steal commodities from their employer, rationalizing that they are underpaid. Or, students who attribute low grades to unfair teachers.

The attempt to prove one's behavior as *rational* and justifiable is a means of proving to oneself that he is worthy of the approval of himself and others.

This defense is common to us all, but the true workaholic really gets tangled up with this one. He must constantly find ways to rationalize the need to work or to keep people in his life thinking he is indispensable. Furthermore, he has to schedule his time to be able to work long hours. So he must always bear in mind the situation and the kind of behavior (isolation) that it requires. Justifying their thoughts and behavior, many workaholics thus ignore the real causes of their anxieties.

The person caught in the work trap needs to deal with the basics of his problem. As long as his thoughts are isolated from his emotions he will continue to be alienated from himself and others.

The workaholic with this problem must forever shift from action back to thinking. Watch how meticulous he becomes. He is involved with reams and reams of details. Even before carrying out a simple act, great mounds of preparation must precede it. Otto Fenichel effectively describes this evasive process when he writes:

> Thinking is preparation for action. Persons who are afraid of actions increase the preparation. In the same way as compulsion neurotics think rather than act, they also prepare constantly for the future and never experience the present.[8]

How true! People who don't live in the NOW but always for the THEN have a severe problem.

The individual who lives primarily inside of his head does not express feelings because he has a fear of expressing them. He is not sure how they will come out because he is not used to dealing with them.

The reactive individual, who is attempting to hide from some deep fear or conflict through his work, does not usually have a great love for his work. Since work serves as a cover-up for feelings, his blocking of them prevents him from feelings at all. Therefore, he enjoys little. He often is a *frigid* person. Observers usually report this characterization of those who fall into the workaholic category.

The avoidance factor against feelings manifests itself in yet another way. Workaholics, more often than not, will develop cold intellects. Through the intellect they develop a counterattack against feared emotions. Instead of letting go emotionally in a situation calling for laughter, this workaholic type may sit in the corner with his arms folded and a scowl on his face. He is defiantly saying, "Just try to make me laugh." In therapy these people, hiding behind their intellectual defenses, will at times produce or reveal emotional material, but they lack the ability to relax in order to consider it objectively. They are usually poor subjects because they resist therapy. They have all the rational answers. They lack the spontaneity to feel. Their feelings are dammed up. All that is left is jargon.

They want to argue with the therapist.

An individual of this type, unaware of his insufficiencies, many times must prove to himself that he is very much in control. "I am an efficient person." "I have a lot on the ball; just look at the amount of work I turn out." This is the rationale with which he defends his overwork. But deep within, such a person is cold and unable to show sympathy toward others. He is an empty shell emotionally.

Rationalization leads to fantasy. The workaholic has created his own fantasies which keep him going. The first fantasy rationalization has to do with the *quantity of work required.* He operates under a delusional system that rationalizes: "The solution to any problem is to work harder and harder at it." "If there is a financial problem, the solution is to get out there and roll up your sleeves and work harder." This is, of course, very faulty thinking.

Jim was a professed workaholic. He learned when he was a child that the most important thing in life was being a responsible person. His parents made him work constantly. In order for him to play baseball with the neighborhood boys he would have to sneak out to do so. In Jim's thinking, work was a virtue, play was a sin. At least that's the message that got through to him from his parents.

Wayne Oates, who quotes Robert Neale from *In Praise of Play,* writes an insightful paragraph on the magical thinking of the typical workaholic in answer to the question: "Why do reasonable men and women become addicted to perpetual work?"

Robert Neale gives an excellent lead toward an answer: it is because we rely on the "magic" of our own clever efforts. He says that the spiritual creativity of life follows a pattern of "new discharge and new design." The response of faith and religion is one of rest and playfulness. Neale says the "magic is the work response" to the spiritual realm of life. By our own clever efforts and works, we seek to outwit our basic nature and that of the universe. Thus magic replaces creativity. The workaholic assumes that everything happens as a result of his efforts and therefore he must work incessantly. His attitude reminds us of that of the rooster, who proudly reminds God each day: "It is I whose crow causes the sun to rise!" With such vain fantasy, the workaholic becomes isolated and overloaded with a false sense of responsibility. "Nobody Knows the Troubles I've Seen" is the frenetic maneuvering of someone temporarily at a loss without his "work magic." [9]

Rationalization is mythical ("magical") thinking and it can upset the balance that leads toward a more fulfilled life. The constant need to work harder may, and often does, become self-defeating.

The second fantasy rationalization which many workaholics use to a great extent is the *need to perform*. One of his underlying rationales is the formula, "What you *do* is more important than who you *are*."

Where does that idea come from? The following may give us a clue.

One recognized workaholic said that the most important event in his household while he was growing up was the bringing home of report cards. A big thing was always made of it. He reported that for days before the grades were to come out he had diarrhea. If he was down in one subject, he would be sorely punished, perhaps by being grounded for some weeks. His parents were never satisfied with average or even above-average grades. He remembers well the time he brought home four As on his report card. The only grade his father commented about was the one B. His father, a civil engineer, and his mother, a socialite, were success driven. Consequently, this man grew up believing that performance was the only thing that counted. He was continually at his studies or using what little leisure time he had to do something that would contribute to the furthering of his education.

We are geared for competition. The losing football team does not generate many fans to watch it play. The company that fails to gain contracts in competition with others is likely to go bankrupt. It is the students with superior records who win the competition for college entrance and graduate schools.

At the occupational level a person may be under considerable pressure to advance and make the increased income often needed to support a family. In general, most of us are encouraged to be ambitious and to think big.

We are told at every level that strict competition leads to greater productivity, an increased sense of purpose, and higher standards of excellence. In many cases this is true. However, inappropriate or indiscriminate competition can ruthlessly destroy a person or hurtfully divide a family or group. It can constantly overload a person's capacities and rob him of vitality and health.

A third fantasy rationalization for many is the *need to be perfect*, growing out of the need for approval.

Many workaholics fear that even the slightest mistake will completely crumble their entire structure of past achievements. Each thing that is done is too important to risk any kind of failure. So one really has to work at it. The risk exists in delegating work to others, because if they fail to carry out the perfected standards, this, too, represents personal failure. Trusting an associate is too great a risk. Nothing can be delegated. This chronic refusal grows out of a basic insecurity which feeds an obsessive fear of failure.

The wish to please one's parents, or to live up to their ideal or ambition, often determines a person's career. One day in a seminary classroom the professor asked members of the class why they had chosen the ministry. Almost one-third said it was because their parents or relatives wanted them to become ministers.

Unless a person develops maturity, the need for approval may become the deepest motivation in choosing a career. The father who wants his son to follow in his footsteps is a common occurrence. In the old world this was the rule, not the exception. In our world presently, this kind of parental hope may cause greater problems, because culturally it is not expected.

The son has the freedom not to comply. If there is not any psychological maturity he may be ruled by a deep fear of displeasing his father.

Dr. Karl Menninger speaks about this problem:

> But we know that beneath the conscious . . . there are unconscious motives which strongly influence any decision. Among these, in the case of vocational choice, one must undoubtedly include the unconscious reaction of the son to his father's attitudes. Where the conscious identification with the father in the selection of the father's profession will appear to be positive, there will be negative valences in the unconscious and vice versa. In other words, a son may select his father's profession, or one that the father wishes him to follow, ostensibly because it flatters and pleases the father; but unconsciously such a son will often be motivated strongly by the repressed impulse to compete with, eclipse, or supersede his father. Similarly many a son who disappoints his father by what appears to be an aggressive rejection of the parental hopes is unconsciously deterred by love of the father, or by the fear of entering into competition with him. It reminds one of that parable of Jesus about the two sons, one of whom said quickly and politely, "I go sir. I do your bidding," but went not; while the other said, "I will not, I refuse to obey," but did.[10]

Perfectionist drives can have a ruthless effect upon one's personality. They allow little freedom or flexibility. Worst of all, they leave one with strong delusions, because those standards are seldom ever achieved.

The workaholic who simply rationalizes in a land of fantasy cuts himself off from a vast part of life.

Wayne Oates puts it well:

> The work addict may be said to have a poverty of objects of attention. He is bound to the automatic perceptions, feelings, and centers of awareness of his job. He cannot see the whole architecture of life because he has

his eye on one brick. Nor can he feel anything except that it is he who holds that brick in place, and that if he did not the whole structure would collapse. Furthermore, he acts as if the whole structure upholds the universe. None of this is so.[11]

Reaction-formation. If repressed feelings threaten to come into our conscious mind from the subconscious, we may try to keep them down by overreacting, opposite to what we truly feel about them. This can be a healthy way of dealing with reality by compensating for weakness in one area by achieving success in another. A person, for example, who is unable to have an active life in sports because he is physically handicapped, may have an unusually strong drive to excel in the field of music.

Again, it may be manifested by people who crusade militantly against loose sexual morals or the evils of alcohol. Often such people have a background of earlier difficulties with such problems themselves, and their zealous crusading appears to be a means of safeguarding themselves against a recurrence of such behavior.

The deception lies in the fact that a person does not have the ability to accept himself as he is. Preventing an accurate self-picture, it also keeps him from realistically working through his problems and leads to rigidity and harshness in dealing with others.

This defense, used in an unhealthy manner, can be most destructive. Highly exaggerated attempts to overcompensate for strong feelings of self-contempt have made some people into dictators, causing untold suffering for millions as that hate is externalized.

People who get caught in the work trap may use this defense in an unhealthy way as well. If they are fearful of getting involved with people they may compensate by directing their energies into work situations. Thus, many managers, to overcome strong feelings of inadequacy, will come on very strong at work, attempting to hide or repress such feelings by appearing to be independent and aggressive. Otto Fenichel discloses how this defense is related to the workaholic:

Examples of the rigidity of reactive traits are the "hard workers" who are under the necessity of working constantly to keep from feeling their unbearable inner tension . . . . It is obvious why work under these conditions necessarily is less effective. In this connection certain "Sunday Neuroses" should be mentioned; the patients become neurotic on Sunday because on workdays they avoid neuroses by a neurotic, that is, reactive type of work. Such people do not flee from something in the objective world that for them means temptation or punishment toward fantasy; they flee, rather from instinctual fantasies toward some "reactive" external reality.[12]

Work as a reaction-formation against some instinctual impulses has other deeper meanings as well. Overwork may also be directly related to the conflicts about self-esteem. Many so-called ambitious people may present this side because they despise themselves for their deep-seated inferiority feelings. Overwork then becomes a need to contradict feelings of inferiority.

Sublimation.   This defense allows us to take our unacceptable feelings and redirect them into useful ways. This lets us drain off some of the tension produced by these frustrated desires, but does not cause the guilt and anxiety that we would feel if we expressed them more directly. We would feel guilty if we yielded to our hostile impulses and hurt someone seriously, but we don't feel guilty about playing football or watching boxing matches and violent TV shows.

Sublimation is a defense that is felt to be socially acceptable. For instance, a Catholic nun who is unable to marry may have a strong desire to bear children. She will sublimate these feelings through great dedication when she teaches children in a parochial school.

This defense, however, can be destructive if it conceals reality by preventing confrontation with the real world and thus denying the true satisfaction that comes through dealing with people in a warm, loving manner.

Many workaholics profess the view that they genuinely and

thoroughly enjoy their work. But when their work drive is done by compulsion, external or internal, it actually gives them no pleasure at all. It becomes a bore, sheer drudgery. The sublimation may have a way of turning back upon itself.

This can be illustrated by the compulsive housewife. She cleans the home to make things pleasant for others and for herself. In this she is manifesting love for others. But at the same time she can, by her aggressive cleaning, attempt to get rid of *all* dirt, which comes to stand for *bad* things. Her continued desire to keep things clean may drive her family "up the wall." What started out to be a pleasurable act now makes everyone miserable because of her compulsive tidying up. The sublimation breaks down and hatred is actually turned against the people she loves. The same is true of the workaholic who uses work as a defense against intimacy or other necessary life responsibilities.

Over the long haul these mechanisms, when used for excessive work, are nonproductive. They serve to block a person from squarely facing problems and people in a warm and loving manner, and thus, emotional growth is thwarted. On the other hand, it can be one of the most rewarding experiences when the workaholic gives up misusing these defenses.

9

Pitfalls for the Unwary

*Every human act could be under-
stood if we knew all the pertinent
facts.*

MYRON is obsessed by his work. His family, friends, and
business associates at times describe him as a robot. Everything he does seems to be mechanical, and he appears to be
consumed by his work.

Jack feels guilty much of the time. Just about everyone can
see it. He walks with his shoulders slumped, his eyes never
focus on yours when you talk with him—a dead giveaway.
He's seldom at home. If you want to reach him, try calling him
at work first.

Phil is highly devoted to his work. He constantly puts himself down with negative remarks about his weaknesses. He
gets angry if members of his family call to ask him to go to a
social function in the evening. He's not much interested in
having fun.

These three typical workaholic types disclose additional
underlying factors behind the work trap not observed in the
last chapter. People become work addicted because they become obsessed with it, are loaded with guilt, and dislike
themselves intensely. Recognizing the defenses used by the
ego to ward off stress is fundamental to an understanding of
the problem. But the person caught in the work trap may be
there because of other unconscious needs as well.

There is a humorous gibe which indicates that psychotics
build castles in the sky, neurotics live in them, and psychia-

trists collect rent on them. Emotional problems seem to be endemic in today's society. It is estimated that one in every ten hospital beds is occupied by someone with such problems. People are finding it more and more difficult to deal with the environmental stresses thrust upon them. It is helpful to note, however, that mental disease or emotional disturbance no longer carries with it the stigma of shame and embarrassment as it did in the past.

A person becomes psychotic when his mental functioning is sufficiently impaired to interfere with his meeting the demands of life. This impairment is due to a serious distortion of reality. Hallucinations or delusions distort reality and an individual's inability to focus may be so profound that his ability to respond appropriately to various situations is grossly impaired.

A neurosis, on the other hand, as noted in the previous chapter, has a different psychological base. Anxiety is the main characteristic evident in the neurotic. Someone has put it this way: "A psychotic believes that $2 + 2 = 5$; a neurotic believes that $2 + 2 = 4$ but can't stand it!" A neurotic does feel anxiety and he will attempt to control it on an unconscious level or automatically deal with it through the use of one or more of the defenses outlined in the last chapter.

"What does all this have to do with the workaholic?" you may ask. Just this: one of the basic themes we are seeking to set forth in this book is that workaholism is a neurotic way some people choose to deal with their deep inner problems. It is obvious that the workaholic is obsessed with and by his work.

Obsessive-compulsive

Workaholics have an obsession—work, work, work—even if they drop dead. What is an obsession? The dictionary indicates that the term *obsession* is a state of being whereby a person is ruled by an idea, desire, or behavior pattern. It is an idea, emotion, or impulse that is repetitive. It is normal if it does not interfere with thinking or behavior, and it is often short-lived.

If a person masks guilt or other anxieties with a form of acting out certain rituals or repeated behavior patterns, he is said to have some form of an obsessive-compulsive neurosis. Thus, in itself it is a psychological defense.

The deeper the neurosis the more difficult it is for the person to stop his thoughts or behavior. A person who manifests this problem will compulsively check three or four or five times to see if he turned off the stove or locked the back door. People will even get out of bed to check some things. They may constantly examine their pockets or purses to make sure their money or papers have not been lost. Some people will compulsively wash their hands dozens of times a day. Baseball players may perform small ritualistic acts on the field, such as routinely touching second base at the beginning of each inning on their way to the outfield. If the person does not perform the act with which he is obsessed in his mind, he feels nervous and uncomfortable. We have all had the experience of having a certain song or tune remain with us all day long. That's a mild compulsion and is not a problem unless it prohibits or prevents us from normal living. If the obsessive man's wife relates a story and twists some of the details or sequence, he will regularly break in and straighten the whole thing out.

Leonard Cammer has written a book dealing specifically with this kind of neurotic problem. He shows that the idea of the obsessive-compulsive is derived from the Greek word *anake,* meaning "fate."

> Signifying, in its archaic sense, that the obsessive-compulsive was bound to the inevitable decrees of his fate or destiny, presumably tied to the control of a demon of sorts, it thus meant that an obsession was a state induced by an evil spirit. The word "obsession" is derived from the Latin *obsidere,* meaning "to besiege."

Following the basic idea from the original Greek, the obsessive personality is in the firm grip of ideas and compulsive behavior. He is besieged by his own addictive and nonrewarding behavior when it comes to intimacy. He has his own peculiar life-style because of the compulsion to ward off underlying negative feelings.

As we tie this to work attitudes, we see that the person who cares only about getting ahead, who is willing to sacrifice everything in his life for what he considers success, is a compulsive neurotic. His neurosis may work to launch and sustain his career, but it works against him when it comes to closeness and intimacy with other persons. The attitude of achieving status and a higher income, of course, is not wrong in itself. But workaholics who have this hang-up are obsessed with it. They become compulsive in seeking to ward off feelings of guilt, fear, or failure.

Have you noticed that some workaholics have a strong instinctual drive to constantly clear everything up? This applies to everything they may do, around the house, at work or wherever they may be. This obsessive quality makes it difficult for them to leave the office or shop with any business unfinished. It is not at all unusual for most of us to leave work to be carried on the next day. But the workaholic can't cope with this, so he has the neurotic need to finish what he has started, even if it means he must hold up supper and family activities—often for hours—with the plea on the telephone to his wife, "I'm sorry, there's nothing I can do about it, I just have to get this finished." *Finishing* is the compulsive ritual.

In addition, there is often the added strain of stubbornness which becomes the habitual combative method in the struggle for the maintenance or the restoration of self-esteem. He may get his car stuck in a ditch. Call the tow truck service? Never! He has to get it out by himself. Or he may get lost. You would think he would ask directions at the next gas station. Nope, he'll work it out by himself.

This kind of person will often stubbornly stay at work as a means to satisfy his self-centered needs. His stubborn nature brings gratification which is required to contradict some anxiety or guilt feeling. But on the other hand, in fighting unconscious hostilities the person with this type of neurosis will generally appear to be a very gentle person.

Sigmund Freud and the psychoanalytic school of psychology term such a person *anal retentive*. This condition comes about early in life when the child had poor toilet training. This kind of person won't let go of anything. He retains most everything. He gets stubborn. He learned this as a child to assert his independence from mother.

Thus the person acts out this symbolic wish by being *tight* in his adult life with money, his feelings, and many other things. He may be very stingy, a hoarder of money and artifacts. Many counselors today reject this theory, but it has enough truth in it for us to give it a serious look.

This concept appears to have some merit when we observe the workaholic. He is stingy about his time; actually, he hoards it up for work. Furthermore, he's extremely retentive when it comes to giving himself to others. He holds himself back by remaining far longer than necessary at his work or with the current task with which he is involved. He just won't give anyone too much of himself.

The compulsive personality suffers from strong aggressive impulses through longtime training. He learns to get completely absorbed in work. This type continues to drive himself in his work and rationalizes that he enjoys it.

Dr. Karl Menninger, in describing this type of person, states:

> Indeed they do enjoy it more than they would enjoy the anxiety that they would suffer if it were not possible for them to express their aggressions in this way. This kind of work, however, is not a true sublimation; or perhaps we should say it is not all sublimation—it is partly compulsion.[2]

By compulsion, Menninger means that a mechanism is used:

> . . . that is no longer an automatic and comfortable conversion of the aggressive energy into useful channels; it is partly a neurotically determined attempt to overexploit this device and thus to overtax it.[3]

The pity is that such a device never works or suffices because the overtaxing creates resentments within the person. The person may begin to complain about overwork and become depressed and self-castigating. After a while, the cloaking of aggression fails.

In addition, there is often the lack of adequate feeling reactions which are induced by isolation. The individual may appear to be completely cold or may reveal certain emotions only when reassuring conditions exist. The struggle for this reassurance becomes a real battleground within the self. The overall aim is to prove that it is valid.

One workaholic constantly typed himself into roles to gain validity. He felt well only when he knew a certain role which he had to play. When at work he would take on one role; "I am a worker." This gave him security while on the job. When at home he would take on another role and tell himself, "Now I am the husband and I have a beloved family." This made him into a robot, lacking spontaneity.

Such defenses are used to avoid having to get close to people. It is much safer to have all the obsessive ideas floating around in one's head than to risk confronting experiences with other people.

That is why many workaholics appear to be intellectual snobs. Work is noble, but when it is overdone it becomes a ritualistic defense against involvement with the hostile, rejecting world outside. Work. Ideas. Ideas. Work. That's their impregnable fortress.

One of the tragedies of the workaholic is that due to his isolation from the real emotional world he is usually caught up in preparations, always working for the future and never being able to experience the present. As a result, he doesn't live in a real world. He experiences the world as did one client who rejoiced in the walk uphill because he thought of the downhill walk coming later, but was always sad on the downhill trip because he would reflect upon a later uphill climb!

The unfortunate thing about the obsessive workaholic is that work is used to hide his feelings from either himself or others. As an avoidance technique it becomes a self-destructive mechanism. He becomes alienated from himself.

Nagging Guilt

"I would feel guilty if I didn't work as much as I do. After all, the boss is here every night." Guilt is what propels some workaholics. Addictive work behavior can often be used as a means of evading this guilt. In such a case the conscience acts as the strap to beat one down; it serves as an emotional lash that conditions one's judgments. For the obsessive personality it rarely lets up. Addictive work allows the person to rationalize, "I'm good and respectable." In this way it relieves the pressure of guilt.

One must bear in mind that guilt conflicts can have a tremendously crippling, hampering, and tormenting effect upon one's life. In fact, this condition can lead to the outbreak of organic illness.

Guilt is the key to compulsive behavior and is a major contributor toward a person's need to work excessively. Guilt can smolder within the recesses of the mind, causing innumerable problems. It can sour one's enjoyment for living, disillusion a person, and humiliate him. Along with hostility, it may be one of the two most significant variables in emotional illness. Guilt can cause fear and anxiety that, in turn, can create a variety of ills, from chronic fatigue to sexual frigidity and drug addiction. Guilt may become so severe and destructive that its torment may lead a person to suicide.

Sigmund Freud thought of guilt as one of the most powerful emotions ruling our lives. We know that guilt is quite necessary to human existence, but when it interferes with an individual's coping mechanism, it can almost totally immobilize him so that it is nearly impossible for him to function.

Guilt is a vital force to help relieve sorrow over having done something wrong, whether it be social, moral, or spiritual. The famous psychologist Allan Fromme has said that guilt feelings are automatically manifested when the conscience is developed. It is that internal *sound system* which continues to signal the differences between right and wrong. Man has been aware of this since God faced Adam in his guilt in the Garden of Eden!

It is true that guilt often has its roots in childhood. If the child has been squelched, shamed, and punished for self-expression or for releasing his emotions, he will learn that it is wrong to express himself.

If the child is shamed for expressing fear, punished for showing anger, and laughed at for expressing love, he will then learn that anger and fear, for example, are bad emotions. Later in life, with these parent tapes whirling inside the head, guilt may be created when there is expression of these emotions.

Guilt is a common emotion. Many workaholics experience it. People often feel guilt and shame about their feelings, even if they don't express them. It can be very painful and cause much anxiety and defensiveness. Schoonmaker sees dependency desires as a basis for guilt.

> Independence is a cherished ideal in America, especially for executives. We are supposed to stand on our own two feet and make our own decisions. We therefore feel ashamed of any desire to lean on other people. Unfortunately, this desire is a basic part of human nature, and everyone feels it from time to time.
>
> Some people accept this desire as natural and feel little or no shame about it, but many others believe it to be a shameful sign of weakness and try desperately to deceive themselves and other people. They present an extremely independent facade; they can't take orders, reject suggestions and advice, and insist on having their own way in everything. By means of these actions such people may conceal their dependence, but they pay a terrible price for their self-deception. They have to keep deceiving themselves, can never relax or take advice. In many cases, they actually ruin their health.[4]

If guilt is indeed back of much of the workaholic's need to work, he needs to come to grips with the truth that he has a poor self-image. Unlike those who seem not to care about what they do, a guilt-ridden workaholic will do almost anything for approval. His long hours prove to those in his world that he is a good person, dedicated to the organization, company, or profession. He is not only attempting to prove these traits to the public but, even more importantly, to himself. The extraneous work becomes a reassuring system which appears to be valid. This gives assurance that he is a conscientious, hard worker. Possibly he needs this positive reinforcement because deep within himself, his ego is sagging. He may feel vastly inferior or inadequate. His hard work becomes the means to dispel such mental attitudes.

He glows when he hears, "My, isn't Bill dedicated? He stayed late again last night to finish the project ahead of time. What a hard worker." Needing approval, the approbation or sanction from others bolsters his spirits and keeps him functioning until the next time. In the meantime, Bill continues to be late every night, and frequently goes to the office on weekends. As a result, he becomes further and further isolated from his wife and children. Soon they will hardly know him.

When the person has no insight into his pathological attitudes, there is little hope of turning his life around. Inconsistency becomes pronounced. He works excessively to gain approval on the one hand. On the other, he loses it with his own family and friends as they begin to resent his isolated behavior.

Destructive Self-hate

When a person feels guilty he will usually not only try to find relief, but he will attempt—at times—to release that guilt through some kind of atoning process. When a person's ego is buffeted by the strong demands of the superego (conscience), often the ego's need for punishment will become secondary to the need for forgiveness. This helps in relieving the pressure of a strong persecuting conscience. The punishment becomes more of a symptom for the more intense general need for absolution.

The individual who uses work to relieve guilt is involved in the absolution phase. It relieves the underlying guilt and therefore the punishment.

Other workaholics use work as a form of self-hate by depriving themselves of any pleasure at all. Thus, work itself becomes the whipping boy or the form of punishment, because such people do not feel worthy of many of life's joys. Because they are angry with themselves they turn the hostility upon themselves.

If you question whether these kinds of people are angry or not, watch them closely. They are more often than not highly anxiety laden. Much of their anxiety may be free-floating. They are not able to readily identify the anxiety nor the root cause for the emotional upheaval. The following quotation is a partial description of a highly stressful individual disclosing much hostility. It aptly describes many men who, for example, need to work excessively to drain off anxiety and hostility.

> . . . if in conversation you frequently clench your fist, or bang your hand upon a table or pound one fist into the palm of your other hand in order to emphasize a conversational point, you are exhibiting stressful   [sic] gestures. Similarly, if the corners of your mouth spasmodically, in tic-like fashion, jerk backward slightly exposing your teeth, or if you habitually clench your jaw, or even grind your teeth, you are subject to muscular phenomena of a continuous struggle . . . .[5]

A person who has anger, much of which is directed toward the self, will build up an idealized image of himself, because he cannot tolerate himself as he actually is. Now it can get very complex. The individual's image often appears to counteract this calamity, but having placed himself on a pedestal, he can tolerate his real self still less and starts to rage against it. He then despises himself and chafes under the yoke of his own unattainable demands upon himself. He wavers between self-adoration and self-contempt, between his idealized image and his despised image. He is left with no solid middle ground to fall back upon.

Dr. Theodore I. Rubin puts self-hate into better perspective when he points out that all neurotic manifestations are incarnations of self-hate and have highly self-destructive elements. Among them are,

Compartmentalization, in which we keep different aspects of our lives separate as if we are separate people and only let parts of ourselves in on other parts of ourselves . . .

Fragmentation, in which we function as separate autonomous parts . . .

Inappropriate and excessive repression, in which we put down and out of consciousness our very own feelings, ideas and thought . . .

Deadening, in which we anesthetize ourselves . . .

Resigning, in which we pull out of involvement with life in its various manifestations . . . .

While these mechanisms may have their earliest origins as attempts to cope with anxiety, they eventually, like Frankenstein's monster, become the source of enormously exaggerated anxiety and misery in themselves.[6]

From what we've learned about workaholics, all of these seem to apply, don't they?

It is very probable that the performance-driven workaholic not only faces the strong possibility of failure because he cannot attain his high standards but also experiences nonfulfillment. The extreme drive to attain and to compete becomes a factor that promotes personal discontent and unhappiness which are forms of self-hate. At a deeper level, this drive prevents closeness. Probably the worst result is that it prevents one from loving himself because of the impossible standards that are set. Genuine joy cannot be attained because the achievement of those impossible goals is never reached. When they are not, there can be no self-acceptance. Without any inward peace and fulfillment, self-hate is perpetuated.

Then an unusual phenomenon takes place. There is formulated a new kind of hatred, hate for hating oneself. This creates more conflict, driving the person toward more work as a redeeming factor, because the person must make every effort to believe that he doesn't hate himself. When this takes place, of course, there can be no self-evaluation or insight. If you ask many true workaholics if they hate themselves, they will act surprised at such a foolish question. "Of course I don't. I'm such a devoted person to my work. After all, look how well I take care of my family and my financial obligations."

A man who has a very strong competitive drive may never see his self-hate because he has been that way as long as he can remember. He is unaware of his lack of spontaneity.

When workaholism is a manifestation of self-hate it actually abets in reducing the person to a machine. A person who is so driven has no opportunity to feel and actually lacks the ability to do so. His hyper-energy becomes directed toward inanimate objects—paper, pen, tools, typewriter, figures, filing cabinets, dictaphone, statistics.

Usually an adjunct to such a state is that the person may more and more develop the inability to make choices, to evaluate, and to grow emotionally. He is reduced to a slavelike status because he is driven by inner compulsions. The feelings of others mean little to him.

The obsessive, the guilt-ridden, and the masochistic person are all to be pitied. The anxiety and problems created because of these existing patterns are sad indeed. Those who really get hurt are the close relatives. When the workaholic uses his work to run from underlying anxieties and problems, they are not usually resolved and the anxiety remains.

Anxiety can induce people to act irrationally and defensively. But, it has a constructive side as well. It can motivate individuals to reach their full potential by assisting them to cope with tensions. Through it individuals can learn, love, and create. An appropriate old proverb states, "The stronger the wind blows, the greater the oak tree becomes."

Alan Schoonmaker makes this comment about the stresses of life:

> Anxiety is inherent in the human condition; it is a result of the pressures of our complex society, and we can never escape it completely. To ignore it or deny it will simply increase its impact on us. And its primary impact is to undermine our most basic right and most basic human quality—our ability to choose. It can bind us to our alter-

natives or prevent us from choosing the ones that will really satisfy us.

The best solution to the problem of anxiety is, therefore, to understand it, for understanding it will develop the power to choose.[7]

Most authorities today agree with a multicausation theory when studying addictive behavior. This includes cultural, biological, and psychosociological factors that interact in a complex pattern. Workaholism falls into the category of addictive behavior. For that reason several factors may go into the underlying causes of why people get themselves into a work trap.

Experts in the field all say there is no such thing as an "addictive personality." Addictive behavior is an outcome of a process of adaptation to an addictive way of life. When we think of causes we must bear in mind that there are high risk cultures which include broken homes, economic deprivation, and exposure to an addictive life. While there is not a basic addictive personality, there are a number of common personality traits. Look for these when you try to relate to a true workaholic. These traits include feelings of inadequacy and low self-esteem, a sense of rejection and alienation, dependence, highly egocentric characteristics, hostility, and aggressiveness.

The authors of this book believe that workaholism is definitely a form of addictive behavior. Therefore, patterns characteristic of other addictions, such as alcohol and drugs, may well be evidenced in those who have the driving compulsion to work unceasingly.

Finally, it should be stated that the border line between emotional health and illness is sometimes difficult to establish. In the same vein, there is no single, all-inclusive reason for the state of workaholism. An occasional manifestation of what appears for the moment to be a characteristic, as set forth in this book, may occur in anyone. The one major difference would appear to be that a person who definitely has an excessive work problem not only possesses certain symptoms, but these symptoms appear to take over and exercise almost absolute control. They disrupt the ongoing process of life because such patterns possess a compulsive inflexibility. Persons with these symptoms seldom have the ability to adjust to the changes in the existing, real world beyond the office or shop.

Part III
The Cures Releasing the Work Trap

10

Never Too Late
for Change

*In a higher world it is otherwise;
but here below to live is to change,
and to be well-adjusted is to have
changed often.*

IT IS one thing to identify a problem and to determine its root
causes. It is quite another to find the solutions to the problem.
It is our desire now to provide what we believe to be some
positive ways for the workaholic to change his behavior and
thus find a more well-rounded and fulfilled life. It is our con-
tention that any person caught in the work trap who really
wants to change can do so.

Easy solutions to difficult problems rarely occur. We do not
propose to take lightly the problems set forth in this book. We
do not wish to offer simplistic answers, but realistic ways to
assist people to get out of the morass in which they find themselves.

To begin with, it is essential to be sensitive to where the
workaholic is coming from. A principle practiced by ancient
Greek fighters was not to cut off the enemy's retreat. They
found that their opponents would fight more desperately
when they were bottled up.

In our modern workaday world we should permit the workaholic a way to save face.

Criticism should begin with praise and honest appreciation
of what the person does well. Then go on to point out how his

problem can be faced and quite possibly be resolved. Compassion and understanding go a long way. These qualities will appeal to him because they reflect an honest desire to be helpful.

Some people, in trying to help individuals caught in the work trap, may write the whole project off. He's-always-been-that-way-and-he-won't-change labels destroy the incentive to reach out to people.

To suggest, "Aren't we all a bit neurotic?" to prevent changing is an avoidance technique. True, you, along with everyone else, have psychological handicaps, but that is no excuse for not dealing with them in yourself or in helping others to face them.

After reading the previous chapters you may have come to think that because of many people's past, it is a hopeless proposition to try to change. "My mother didn't love me," or "My parents really messed me up," are phrases often used by people to explain their present emotional condition. Such rationalizations are often avoidance techniques which inhibit change. "Well, there's nothing I can do about it because of my upbringing, or my past," can become a cop-out against having to alter one's life.

We advocate the importance of looking at the past because people bring the past into the present, but we must not insist that this is the only key in helping people to mature. Present behavior can be changed, regardless of what has happened historically.

Albert Ellis,[1] who leads the Rational Emotive school, points out that some people will avoid change because of the hopeless view that early childhood experiences *must* continue to *control* them and determine their emotions and behavior!

Ellis believes that the strong belief in the continuing importance or significance of the past is illogical for several reasons:

1. By believing this you commit the logical error of overgeneralization. For example, because your father was unkind does not mean that all men are equally unkind and that you have to use defenses against them all.

2. By allowing yourself to be too strongly influenced by past events, you cease to look for alternative solutions to problems.
3. By remaining influenced by the past you will maintain what the psychoanalysts call "transference" effects—meaning that you will inappropriately transfer your feelings about people in your past life to those around you today. This is, of course, self-defeating.
4. Accepting the influences of the past amounts to your being thoroughly unrealistic in many instances since the present is not the past but usually significantly differs from it. Treating your wife the same way that you treat your mother may, because she definitely is not your mother, easily bring trouble.[2]

If we can release the hold of some of these irrational ideas, recovery and change can indeed take place. As we discovered in the chapters dealing with basic underlying psychological causes, workaholism in itself in most cases is a defense against present anxiety which may have been a learned response early in life. Recognizing that we do not need to be bound to the past can give a person a great lift and encouragement. There is hope because the past has no magical or automatic effect on the present.

Thus, when it comes to solutions, it is not always necessary to know where it all began, but to learn how to stop self-defeating behavior today!

Another important thing to remember when we speak about change and solutions to the problem of workaholism is that every facet of the problem does not have to be changed. In terms of human behavior, we do not have to dwell on numerous emotional problems or try to change many facets of our personality. This gives great hope in dealing with any problem. Often, when one variable is changed, others automatically will be corrected.

There is another important consideration when seeking to find solutions. Bear in mind that you cannot be remade entirely. Actually, no one is asking you to be. Remember, your current problems are due to multiple causes which possibly go back to the early moments of life. It is obviously impossible to dig them all out.

Your personality is always expanding. It is constantly in a state of transition. That is why you need to focus more on the present than on the past. Whatever the conditioning and influences of the past, you can't go back and change them. With professional help you may work through some of the more traumatic or dramatic conflicts of the past, but the supremely decisive fact is what is taking place existentially, in the here and now. You can remodel your traits, habits, and behavior in drastic ways in the present moment. You can then begin to function and be a more fulfilled person in the future.

If you can make a beginning to alter your life where it breaks down, you will discover your motivation toward change increasing. You will come to realize the serious threats of social exclusion, sexual failure, problems on the job, and psychological pain. You will be more aware and you will realize that your maladaptive traits are screaming out to you that you are a loser when it comes to the more basic things of life, in the area of personal relations.

The first step toward effecting change is for the afflicted workaholic to admit that he has a problem. Then he should decide which kind of workaholic he is in order to set goals and change those attitudes which have brought irrationality into his life.

Further, when it comes to changing behavior, it is good to keep in mind that there are five basic ways to bring about change. (1) There must be a *proper climate*. A person must recognize that he has a problem and identify it. (2) There must follow a *strong willingness* and *desire to change*. This has to come from deep within. (3) *Goals must be set* which are not too lofty, but attainable. A good thing to remember here is that "life by the yard is hard, by the inch it's a cinch." (4) *There must be incentive*. The question must be asked, "What's in it for me?" This will help provide proper motivation if the person can answer that question. (5) *Feedback from others* is important in effecting change. People will change more quickly if they get positive strokes from others. What others think will often be the very thing that initiates change.

In seeking solutions, look at three S's that must be changed: A weak spiritual life, wrong views of success, and deficient work satisfaction.

Spiritual Problem

We believe that workaholism, whether you're an agnostic, a Baptist, Presbyterian, Episcopalian, Catholic, Jew, or whatever religion you embrace, is basically a spiritual problem. Any condition, including addictive behavior, that destroys the individual or society goes back to spiritually based deficiencies.

Addictive behavior is a spiritual problem, as we've seen. It produces an imbalance in an individual. Workaholism falls into this category. It is a spiritual problem because it represents escape, destruction of relationships and becomes a substitute for the spiritual vacuum experienced by many people who do not have a vital relationship with Almighty God.

The Bible has much to say about deviant or misguided behavior. It commands changes where human behavior is nonproductive or destructive. "Let him that steals, steal no more." People who are workaholics often become so because of some spiritual defect in their personal lives. Life for them breaks down at some point or other. They use work as a means of escape or as the only way to find fulfillment. One can seek many things to fill the emptiness—money, material possessions, position, creature comforts, fame, respect, admiration, social success, or a job.

The Word of God sets forth spiritual principles that are timeless, even though its words were written thousands of years ago. Those truths have been universally communicated. They work. They are relevant for man's eternal search for meaning and purpose in all areas of life.

The person caught in the work trap needs to heed, for example, the admonition of Scripture, "Keep thy heart with all diligence; for out of it are the issues of life" (Proverbs 4:23). He has narrowed his diligence mainly to one area of life—work—without realizing that he must apply himself in diligence to all areas of responsible living.

The Bible further states, "Happy is the man that findeth wisdom . . ." (Proverbs 3:13). A wise person is one who is reflective. He is a rational person recognizing his faults. He is one who knows he is responsible for his actions. He is one who learns from his failures and takes action to eliminate them as best he can.

The workaholic, without knowing it, has fallen into the trap created by his own society. For many it is a way of life. He needs to reevaluate his life and behavior, choosing to stand above the negative standards set forth by his culture and world. The Bible again has something to say at this point: "Don't let the world around you squeeze you into its own mould . . ." (Romans 12:2 PHILLIPS). For a person to stand up against the standards practiced by those around him, he needs spiritual insight and the strength of the Lord to surmount such obstacles.

The Apostle Paul, in the first century, set forth in his letter to the church in Galatia the marks of a mature spiritual person. He said, "But the fruit of the Spirit is love, joy, peace, patience, kindness, goodness, faithfulness, gentleness, self-control; against such things there is no law" (Galatians 5:22–23 NAS).

The workaholic runs directly counter to several of these characteristics. One that stands out is self-control. He is out of control, at least in one area. He does not control his work. It controls him. He does not experience it in a balanced manner as this verse suggests is the proper standard for a truly balanced and committed spiritual man.

The greatest example for us, of course, is Jesus Christ, the perfect Son of God. He walked our earth for only thirty-three years, three of which were directly spent in ministry. His work was the most important in the universe—doing good, proclaiming the truth of God, and redeeming sinful mankind. Yet He kept things in perfect balance. He was never in a rush, always finding the needed time to relax.

Finally, one biblical admonishment especially apropos for the workaholic is the strong command issued by an ancient prophet to the king of Judah, ". . . Thus says the Lord, 'Set your house in order . . .' " (2 Kings 20:1 NAS).

The workaholic needs to do that!

Redefine Success

Most workaholics have distorted views of what success is. A major solution is to have their views adjusted regarding it. Because workaholics are work-achievement oriented, they are consumed with ambition beyond a reasonable point.

Too strong an ambition can lead to a presumptuousness that is destructive. Work becomes everything. Ambition is much like the basic physical drives of the body. Love, sex, hunger, and thirst are neither wrong nor right in themselves. But too much of any of them can lead to severe problems. Ambition is much like that. It is a normal drive, but it is possible for it to be misdirected.

The thing to look for is the underlying motives that prompt ambition. A person must first look at the rightness of the goal. Then he must examine the motive for reaching that goal.

If you are simply measuring success by the amount of money you earn, or your status or prestige, then quite possibly your motives are wrong. Workaholics frequently have a strong drive to achieve. In principle, it is a fine goal. In practice, it is not so easy to find the proper balance with the rest of life. Dr. Gary Collins, a noted Christian psychologist, speaks about the drive for success:

> One of the major reasons for stress at work is the idea, ingrained in our thinking, that work is a measure of our self-worth. This is especially true of males. To justify our existence and prove to ourselves that we are valuable people, we assume that we must succeed on the job. If we don't succeed at work, so the myth goes, then maybe we aren't worth much as persons. So we start pushing to get ahead, hardly pausing to realize that when one person moves ahead, someone else gets pushed aside.
>
> When I was in graduate school, we learned that it was important to be successful. It wasn't always stated

explicitly, but the implication was that in order to be successful as psychologists we had to prove our worth by writing articles or books, by achieving fame and status, and by earning enough money so that we could live an obviously affluent lifestyle. Since graduation I have watched many of my colleagues push to be successful and to demonstrate all these marks of vocational accomplishment. Too often, however, broken marriages, ulcers, excessive drinking, and discouragement have come along as by-products of this great push to get ahead.[3]

Persons who have this problem need to drastically change their philosophy of success. They need to reestablish their achievement-orientation about life as the dominant motivation for work. And, at the same time, the desire to move up in an organization should be deemphasized if the drive militates against a balanced life-style. It is good that a few firms today emphasize performance instead of promotion, but they are a small number compared to the many who are fearful of violating tradition.

As we have stated several times earlier, an individual can be a success at work but be a miserable failure as a husband, father, or friend. There are many definitions of success. Among others, one definition is working to the maximum of our potential at any given point in time. But it also encompasses the idea of a total life experience. Bessie Anderson Stanley, in *What Constitutes Success*, is close to our view: "He has achieved success who has lived well, laughed often, and loved much." It is not necessarily based upon high performance and certainly not on perfection. It is interesting to note, for example, that a baseball hitter is considered a success if he hits .300. All hitters aspire to this goal. Yet think of it in another way. A hitter is a success if he fails 70 percent of the time!

Another unrealistic standard often accepted is that success is measured by the *vertical line*. Anytime a person has moved up in the business world he is considered a success. If this happens he will be honored by his peers. But we must remember that success is never attained by the heights one reaches, but by the obstacles one has to overcome to attain those heights.

The authors are completely convinced that in the final analysis the bottom line of success must and always will include God in one's life. The most important thing in the world is "not to make a living but to build a life." This cannot be done without permitting the Lord to have a rightful place in a person's life. Never underestimate the truth that God is intensely interested in your success. The Bible deals with money and possessions in over a thousand passages. Transcending any ideas about material goods or status in the world of commerce is the view that a person must be right with God if he is to be successful.

Meaningful work may not necessarily be the most financially rewarding. Rather, it is that *kind* of work that is the most satisfying to *you* and provides a genuine sense of achievement. Meaningful work is the kind that does not lock you in but enhances your opportunity to relate to the world. Seeking only money and prestige won't cut it, for they far too often leave you feeling alienated and useless.

Wallace Johnson, the pioneer executive in the development of Holiday Inns, puts this in perspective when he comments about being a success:

> Success is stopping trying to do everything yourself. From the moment I stopped trying to accomplish everything with my own resources and let God guide me, things were different. I got better ideas. Names of people to see, places to go, new ideas just popped into my mind. Ideas are the great values in this world, and suddenly I was filled with them.

We heard recently about a thirty-two-year-old New York millionaire who wants more out of life than a fancy house, trips around the globe and a well-endowed bank account. What's he doing? Going to medical school to become a physician. He said that he found the business world stimulating, but he was not getting the deepest satisfaction from it because it did not provide the end goal of a lifetime.

He found that simply making a lot of money did not afford him the ability to develop fully as a person because success is a very personal thing. "I'm looking for *success as a human being*," he has stated.

The workaholic must be aware that working long hours at a job does not necessarily spell success. It is so often found in other avenues of life, as the young millionaire has begun to experience.

Reassess Work Satisfaction

Another solution is for the workaholic to reevaluate his job so that it becomes meaningful work. Disregarding social responsibility for the sake of seeking advancement will only aggravate the situation. Career planning requires that a person look seriously at all phases of his life, with the hope of satisfying not only one aspect, but all.

A great part of your life is spent working. It therefore makes sense to get as much fulfillment out of it as possible. Do you feel sometimes as though your job is a dead end? Do you wake up in the morning, thinking about the mountain of work to be tackled and suddenly feel exhausted even before you walk out of the house? If so, you may be suffering from "professional burnout," a syndrome which can strike businessmen, professionals, factory workers, housewives, or anyone else locked into a job.

In talking about "burnout," Dr. LeRoy Spaniol, a Boston University professor, describes it as "a sense of dead-endedness, a feeling that you have nowhere to go, that nothing new is happening." [4] It may be accompanied by such symptoms as weariness, irritability, migraine headaches, and backaches.

Spaniol says that burnout occurs because people ignore their own needs by trying to be Spartan, often literally working until they drop. He believes that some of the ways of combating burnout range from exercising to setting sensible work goals to talking out problems with people who can help, rather than bottling up frustrations. Among other things, the reconditioning of work habits and attitudes can lead to a more enriched and fulfilled life. This, in turn, prevents burnout and job dissatisfaction.

Another problem which may decrease job satisfaction is inability to delegate work to subordinates. The workaholic has difficulty either because of his own perceived importance, with accompanying mistrust in the abilities of others, or because he is afraid to delegate due to his poor self-esteem.

If this is a problem, it will take some good hard work to overcome. Delegation may be easy to write or talk about; it is quite another thing to perform. If only the workaholic could gain the insight into the derived benefits of learning how to delegate, it will ease job pressure considerably, increase time for other important and broader functions on the job, and will, in time, increase the chances of advancement because it frees him to develop other skills which will be of greater worth to him and his employer.

When considering solutions, it is well to learn the *how to*'s. Much literature in the management field is available to assist in delegating. Boiled down, there are six main principles of delegation. They are:

1. Select the jobs to be delegated, and get them organized for turnover.
2. Pick the proper person for the job.
3. Prepare and motivate the delegate for his assignment.
4. Hand over the work, and make sure it is fully understood.
5. Encourage independence.
6. Maintain supervisory control—never relinquish the reins.[5]

In order to effectively begin to delegate, the workaholic needs to identify the reasons why he finds it so difficult. Here is a partial list:

1. He feels he can do it better than anyone else.
2. He feels insecure about the job or about himself as a person.

3. He feels he may be disliked.
4. He feels mistrust for other people.
5. He feels everything has to be perfect, not allowing mistakes in others.
6. He feels inadequate in knowing how to balance workloads.
7. He feels a failure in knowing how to administer responsibility.
8. He feels a lack of competence in explaining, controlling, and following-up.

Finally, successful workers find that there is as much—or more—satisfaction from doing a job well as from contemplating the finished product. Far more real than completion and prestige is the stimulation that arises from the sense of accomplishment. When this value is accepted, it will affect one's way of behaving and thinking. Personal, inner rewards follow.

Developing one's *spiritual* life, redefining the meaning of *success,* and seeking greater work *satisfaction* will go a long way toward making that a reality.

11

Working Through
the Problem

*If you want to make the world a
better place, start with yourself.*

IT IS important for the recognized workaholic to follow a
strategic plan for his life, not only for the present, but for the
future as well. A five-year-old youngster was overheard saying, "God made a lot of days in a year so we wouldn't try to do
everything at once." A wise statement! Those caught in the
work trap are far too often guilty of trying to squeeze too much
activity into too short a duration of time.

Learn Better Ways to Cope With Stress

Following are several practical and helpful steps one can
follow to obtain relief from stressful situations. See if you can
add to the list.

First, ability must be accepted for what it is. Stress is often
created because one has a reputation to live up to or he has the
feeling that he must excel at some particular thing.

As Socrates wisely stated, we should know and understand
ourselves, our gifts, our abilities. "Know thyself" was the
theme of the ancient Greek society. We, therefore, must learn
to recognize our limitations. This is an important concept.

Second, many of us need to develop wider interests in life.
Stress is frequently a by-product of a lack of interest in the
broader areas of satisfying living. We need to allow for the

development of the creative drive within ourselves.

Diversification is a great aid in relieving stress.

Third, we must learn how to accept the fact that our work is really never completed. This fact keeps us going and adds zest to our living. This can lead to "hurry sickness," causing stress. The need to complete the particular job or task at hand and failure to do so immediately often leads to self-castigation and harassment. If this is a problem for you, recognize and accept the fact that life itself is a series of unfinished events and uncompleted processes. So is work.

Fourth, we must learn how to drain off the built-up energy created by stress. The reduction of this tension can be handled in various ways. Instead of anger, frustration, and other nagging feelings being repressed or acted out in our work, they need to be expressed in other ways. Exercise is certainly one of the better ways to reduce tension. More will be said about this in a later chapter.

Someone has rightly said that stress never leaves you where it consumed you. It will always render some change within you. It will either make you more frustrated, weaker, tougher, harder, colder, or angrier, or it will turn you into a softer, gentler, more understanding human being. The way you deal with stress many times helps determine your future.

Many workaholics are yes-men. They are bound by others' wishes, commands, or approval for reasons already discussed. Learning to say no is a strong step in the right direction when a person already overloaded with work and responsibility allows added responsibility to be thrust upon him. There are at least four basic ways to assert oneself when objecting to accepting overloads or taking on extra work: (1) say no; (2) say no with a truthful reason; (3) say no with a "maybe next time" answer; (4) say no with an excuse.

Some people believe that being assertive means to be strongly aggressive. This is wrong. Assertiveness means that the individual can maturely discuss intelligently and openly his true opinions and feelings without overreacting.

A popular clergyman in Southern California was asked to address a ministerial group in a large city. The topic requested was, "How a Minister Can Learn to Say No." The response of

this busy clergyman in his letter of reply was one word—
"No!" He has learned the art well.

Challenge Your Negative Self-image

Lack of self-esteem is a root cause for addictive or maladaptive behavior. The president of a large American corporation
believes that a good, healthy self-image is the most vital factor
he looks for in people who seek to join his firm.

> The first thing I look for is a sense of personal worth. It's
> a subjective quality and hard to define, but I generally
> know it when I see it. These individuals are decent, hon-
> est and by their nature inspire confidence in others. They
> reflect self-respect and a belief in themselves.[1]

It takes a person with self-worth to be capable of treating
others so as to gain and retain their respect and affection. This
is the sort of person who, instead of climbing over his fellow
workers whom he has pulled down, sets himself to help
everyone around him in order that he may move up with them.

It is important for the workaholic to develop a strong sense
of his individuality. This is not to be confused with isolation or
the uniqueness of standing alone, or refusing to interact with
others. It is the process of interaction. This is a mark of maturity, the ability to relate or deal with others when there is
anxiety or conflict.

Psychologists agree that a person's mental picture of himself
can be changed. He may be unaware of his deficiencies, but
one is never too old to change his self-image through self-
analysis. As we become more familiar with our inadequacies
and our needs and attempts to change, we learn to better understand other people.

Because people have marked individual differences there is
not one set approach that will work for everyone. However,
one thing is necessary for all change—the *will* to change. The
workaholic must face up to his detached life and see the results of such behavior not only within himself but in the lives
of those around him.

Now that you have recognized the need to change here are a

few things which will help you facilitate the change:

1. Don't allow yourself to indulge in guilt and shame.[2]
2. Look for the causes of your behavior within your current situation and not in personality defects within yourself.[3]
3. Remind yourself that there are alternative views with every event. This attitude will enable you to be more tolerant in your interpretation of others' intentions and more generous in dismissing what might appear to be their rejection of you.[4]
4. Don't allow others to criticize you as a person; it is your specific actions that are open for evaluation and improvement. Accept constructive feedback graciously if it will help you.[5]
5. Remember that failure and disappointments are sometimes blessings in disguise which tell you that your goals were not right for you, or that your effort wasn't worth it.[6]
6. Do not tolerate people, jobs, and situations which make you feel inadequate. If you can't change them or yourself enough to make you feel worthwhile, walk out on them or pass them by. Life is too short to fill it with "downers." [7]
7. Enjoy feeling the energy that other people transmit, the unique qualities and range of variability of other fellow human beings. Imagine what their fears and insecurities might be and how you could help them. Decide what you need from them and what you have to give. Then let them know that you are open to sharing with them.[8]
8. Accept the truth that God sees a great deal of worth in you. He has made it possible for you to be redeemed and to become a child in His forever family!

Throw Off the Yoke of Guilt

In chapter 9 we discovered that work can be a defense mechanism or a means of seeking to wash out guilt. The workaholic needs to evaluate his guilt feelings and deal with them in a direct manner, rather than use environmental conditions as a whipping boy either to punish himself or as an escape. To relieve oneself of guilt a person must evaluate whether he needs some special insights or distinguish between reasonable or unreasonable demands placed on himself. The acceptance of one's failure, without continually experiencing guilt, will go a long way toward healing. And, thank God, forgiveness, by God's grace, is constantly available to us!

One of the strange things recognized by behavioral scientists is that frequently those who are hit the hardest by guilt are those who have the least reason to be affected by it.

This reveals that knowing how to handle inappropriate guilt can give us much relief from suffering both emotional problems and psychosomatic illnesses.

For a person to find relief for guilt, he should first seek forgiveness through the grace of God offered through His Son. The Cross of Christ is God's way of pardoning us when we accept His provision for forgiveness by faith.

Both religion and psychology are concerned with making men whole. There can be no wholeness or great change within a person without the dissipation of guilt. Both serve in helping to identify and to relieve guilt. They must cooperate.

Many people, after seeking spiritual forgiveness, continue to be laden with psychological guilt. They may hold on to nagging feelings about something they did years ago. Or, they may blame themselves unjustly for something for which they were not responsible, thus leading to false guilt.

When guilt has been identified, a healing process can begin. This little procedure may help you to rid yourself of it:

- Write the guilt down on paper.
- Confess it to God.
- Talk to someone about it.
- Throw the paper away and forget the conversation!
- Accept the forgiveness God provides.

Get Close to Those You Love

Intimacy avoidance is a hallmark of the workaholic. The reason he is often oblivious to needs is that he denies the

presence of need in others. This makes him oblivious to opportunities to satisfy that need. It is like a person who denies
the reality of pain; he is often unaware of the source of the
pain.

The fear of getting close to others is behind intimacy avoidance. The workaholic needs to take a good look at this. "Am I
using my work to avoid dealing with people or conflicts in my
personal life?" If so, he needs to seek and to find solutions that
will change his relationships. It may be difficult at first to
discover this about yourself, but healing will not take place
until you do something about it. Facing reality may not only
be uncomfortable, but you may be confronted with the necessity of taking positive action which—you may fear—will be
hazardous and disagreeable because it will force you to open
up.

Avoiding change and close involvement in the personal
lives of those we love come down to one thing: a lack of concern for others' welfare.

The workaholic needs to strengthen his personal relationships and seek a balance between work and friends. A person
who desires to discipline his life can have the best of both
worlds—satisfying personal relationships and meaningful
work.

To break down the bars of the "prison of aloneness" one
needs some relationships which exist primarily for themselves. By that we mean selecting relationships where the
emphasis is on the relationship itself rather than on its effects
on the job or career.

To do this a person must be honest and open. This naturally
involves the risk of being hurt. Because the risks are high, it is
important at the outset in this type of relationship to decide
how much you need the other person. Without this understanding you may be unwilling to pay such a price. In this type
of relationship, do not hurry the process.

The workaholic who is unable to relate to people because of
his emotional isolation must be nursed back to health. He
needs to be drawn out of that isolation with compassion and
understanding, by making him realize that life cannot be lived

in an impersonal manner if it is to be meaningful and fulfilling. In manufacturing, transportation, trading, finance, and all other areas of production and commerce, as well as in social life, we deal with people who have the desire for esteem, affection, and understanding.

No person can truly do his best work or attain success in business without the concurrence of others. Facing the human equation and solving it satisfactorily are urgent needs imposed upon workers in all walks of life.

When a person realizes this he will recognize two truths: we are all different and often we are not aware in what respect, to what degree, and why we are different. He will then go out of his way to encourage others to talk about themselves and their interests. He will also recognize that communication is a two-way street and will, as a result, better communicate.

The art of getting along with people has been subject matter for thousands of years. Yet all these years and words have found no substitute for the four virtues of consistency, sincerity, courtesy, and friendliness.

In addition, it is well to remember that the person who gets along with people focuses on strengths rather than weaknesses, and on abilities rather than disabilities. Everyone has problems and everyone is lacking in some quality. We need not despair about these, but positively help solve and overcome them.

Good men are not quick to take offense. They measure criticism by the value there is in it for them, as a guide to doing something better, and not by the degree in which the criticism hurts.

If you use work to avoid closeness, it is wise to change the pattern. Begin working on intimacy with someone who is close to you—wife, daughter, brother. This will aid you in your growth development with others and will bring healing for the body and soul. Leonard Cammer puts it this way:

> Intimacy demands the use of singularly human behavior, nature's gift of speech. Intimacy brings you out of your anatomical shell to reveal your thoughts. When you

verbalize whatever threatens you, your loyal champion closes ranks and helps you withstand it.

Intimacy lets you know your priceless worth to your mate. It gives you courage and fortitude. It expands your ego.

Intimacy reconciles differing likes, efforts, talents and concepts.

Intimacy eddies out and touches others with the lambency of your love . . . intimacy gives you completion.[9]

How liberating it is to be open to other human beings without the need to hide or shut off feelings. Few things are as essential to a lasting intimate relationship as the ability to verbalize feelings. Mind reading is a game many engage in, but it will not do in many situations. If you can't express feelings, you will rarely find understanding with the other person.

What must be done? These may sound like simple solutions, but it will take hard work to reach this scale of intimacy if you have been used to avoiding it for years.

First, you have to convince yourself that improvement is necessary. Your relationships are either moving you closer or farther away from others.

Next, you need to accept not only yourself but also your intimates just as they are. Acceptance will help to allow the power of love to work. Then will follow openness so that two people can communicate and listen to each other without fear.

Here are some paths to explore:

1. Listen to your feelings; try to identify what they are.
2. Practice expressing them to those close to you.
3. Set aside special times to communicate more with those with whom you are intimate.
4. Recognize that your job will never totally satisfy you.
5. Give up any notion that your intimate has to live up to your *idealized* expectations.
6. Stop attempts to *remake* the other person.
7. Work out compromise solutions when there is conflict.
8. Be aware that mate-neglect adds up to self-neglect.

9. Seek fresh interests in life with your intimate. Plan time together.
10. Show greater appreciation for others around you.
11. Be aware of the sensitivities in others.
12. Work on meaningful giving and receiving.
13. Seek to show more affection.
14. Accept within yourself an increasing sense of responsibility for your own actions and feelings.
15. *Think* success in your intimate relationships.

In order to learn to grow as a person you may need a trained counselor. Learning to cope with stress, developing assertiveness, changing a negative self-image, throwing off the yoke of guilt, and creating intimate relationships is not an overnight process. Reading books is not the total answer either, although we highly recommend this as a good starting point. Praying and going to church may not always produce these changes, because a religious experience, as important as it is, can also serve as an avoidance defense, to cover over having to deal squarely with problems. Many religious people think that somehow their conflicts will just magically go away if they practice certain rituals.

One of the basic advantages of professional counseling is that it allows for feedback from an impartial individual. Illusions and fantasies about oneself are highly destructive. That is why it is important to find a counselor who understands the defense structure of the ego.

For example, if you answer yes to any of these questions, the chances are you may want to seek professional assistance:

1. Do you think about suicide?
2. Are you highly accident prone, especially at work?
3. Do you have phobias that seriously interfere with your work?
4. Do you often find yourself crying at work?
5. Do you frequently get paralyzed by anxiety attacks at work?
6. Are you addicted to drugs or alcohol?

7. Do you feel excessively guilty on weekends, wishing it were Monday so you could return to work?
8. Do you find it difficult to make decisions at your work?
9. Do you have few close friends?

A good counselor will assist the person in discovering his self-image. A person who rejects himself will also reject others. Jesus said, "Love thy neighbor as thyself." Good, warm relationships begin with a healthy self-image. To help a person understand himself is, therefore, a primary goal of therapy.

In therapy a person is allowed total freedom to communicate what he probably cannot discuss with any other person—attitudes, fears, values, feelings, and desires. Regardless of what he hears, a good counselor will remain nonjudgmental in the sense that he accepts the person for *who* he is, not *what* he does or thinks.

Make sure above all else that your professional counselor is astute enough to know if your behavior is adaptive or maladaptive and be able to treat it as such. It is important that your counselor seek to modify your behavior in the present. Simply working with the past will be costly financially and may lead toward deeper frustrations.

We are convinced that if the workaholic will use whatever means it takes to free himself from the tyranny that binds him, he will have a new perspective on life which will greatly broaden his range of interests and will release him to be more sensitive to other people's needs. This he will find to be far more satisfying and rewarding than the path of overwork which he has chosen to deal with some of his basic problems.

12

Out of the Work Trap

Almost everyone works compulsively at times. The trick is learning to taper off before addiction sets in.

A HUMORIST once asked, "What's the hardest thing in the world to do?"

"I don't know," was the reply.

"It's doing nothing," responded the jokester, "because you can't stop and rest."

The individual caught up in the work trap wouldn't know anything about that because he has trouble just doing nothing.

Unfortunately, relaxation for most workaholics is almost a foreign concept. They can hardly grasp its meaning, let alone learn how to practice it. A striking illustration typifies the problem.

A confessed workaholic had a plush office in the large firm where he was employed. An upholsterer was called in to redo the chair at his desk. The workman pointed out a most interesting thing. Only the front edge of the chair was worn. The man had never learned how to relax.

Those who have served in the Armed Forces undoubtedly remember vividly the rigors of discipline, the long marches, the standing, perhaps for hours, at parade rest. Most welcome were the words uttered by the commanding officer or sergeant, "At ease, men!" The tired muscles, the taut legs suddenly became limp. What welcomed relief, at long last. Life is that way. A change of pace is absolutely vital to prepare one for the next step, the next task, the next day's work. The workaholic frequently doesn't heed the commands and needs of his tired body and mind. Either he is deaf to them or the words "at ease" spell something different in his vocabulary of life.

Many people in the work trap are not aware of their rigorous way of life. They do not recognize that their level of fitness is low, nor do they realize the necessity to stop their present hectic pace. After all, as one observer puts it, they are locked into an existence of five dimensions. The American work day consists of showering, getting into a metal box, going to work, sitting, and then returning home in the same metal box.

There are many illustrations that tell the sad tale of those who are unable to let up and find a suitable change of pace from the pressures of the workaday world.

Ralph was a man in his early sixties who had huge holdings. He was a manufacturing tycoon. His wealth meant little to him. In fact, if you asked him, he could not tell you how much he was really worth.

In therapy Ralph continually complained about how much he was suffering. He constantly assured the counselor that no one, not even his wife, had any idea of how much he was going through. As he talked, it was not uncommon for his heart to race rapidly and for him to perspire profusely. He reported that he had a constant tingling about his body, especially his chest and upper arms. He had been to a number of doctors. He had taken the treadmill heart test. No one was able to diagnose his problem or to help him.

When his wife came in for a consultation she disclosed his life-style in more depth. She revealed that he frequently spoke as though he were on the verge of a nervous breakdown. She indicated that he ate well, was a chain smoker, and his whole life was regulated from the word *go*. His day was marked out in increments of half hours. If there was any deviation, he became extremely irritated with those around him, as well as with himself. He complained that his family was not concerned with him or about his health. They were less than sympathetic, telling him the illnesses were only in his head.

For twenty years he took every new challenge as a means to

run roughshod over people. He took up golf, and practiced for hours until he perfected several facets of the game. It was his deep passion to master everything he attempted. But the tragedy with this man was that he turned even his play into drudgery. He made people weary just noticing his obsession to conquer and master.

You see, Ralph's problem was that he still had fantasies carried over from childhood. As a boy he never dared to play ball or get involved in typical boyhood activities. His father constantly reminded him to "get busy."

He got busy all right, but what a price he had later to pay. He could not relax for relaxation's sake. Now semi-retired, there were no friends and time hung heavily on his hands. He became sick and began to find fault with everyone. Increasingly depressed, all of life became negative. A cloud of gloom and doom hovered over him.

All the energies he had used to develop a great manufacturing firm were now turned in another direction, bent toward self-destruction. Cynical, hateful, and continually negative, he turned on everyone. Driven by the need to master, he never really learned how to live a full and productive life. Relaxation, what there was of it, was only a means in itself, never an end.

Leisure time and relaxation can well serve as one solution for the workaholic looking for his way out of the work trap. It is important to bear in mind that the role of physical rest is a fundamental concept to be understood if the individual is to maximize his efficiency as a properly functioning person. The Bible clearly sets forth the principle of the need to cease from labor. The first book of the Bible discloses its importance. Like God, man needs cessation from labor (Genesis 2:1–4). One of the Ten Commandments reminds us not to forget the Sabbath. God Himself ceased and rested from His creative activity and passed on to His creation the same important principle.

Jewish tradition emphasizes the importance of the Sabbath principle. One writer asks, "What did the world lack after the six days' toil? Rest. So God finished His labours on the seventh day by the creation of a day of rest, the Sabbath"

(Midrash). The sanctity of rest is thus initiated.

By keeping the Sabbath, the rabbis state, man testifies to the belief in God as the Creator of the universe; in a God who is not identical with nature, but is a free personality. The Talmudic mystics said that when the heavens and earth were being called into existence, matter was getting out of hand, and the Divine Voice had to resound, "Enough . . . so far and no further." Man, made in the image of God, has been endowed with creative power too, though limited. In his little universe he has to be able also to say, "Enough . . . so far and no further."

Thus the principle of rest is a reminder of man's potential victory over all material forces that would drag him down. It is a standing reminder that man can emancipate himself from the slavery of his worldly cares, that man was made for spiritual freedom, peace, and joy. The premier Jewish prophet of the eighth century B.C. said that the Sabbath was a "delight" (Isaiah 58:13).

The ancient Hebrews knew the importance of rest. The Sabbath was set aside out of thanksgiving for the achievement of work. Time was needed at the end of the work week to pause and find a needed change of pace. The early Christians carried on the tradition of Israel. Sunday, the first day of the week, was considered the Lord's Day. It was reserved for gladness and rest.

Those early Christians also took their cue from their Lord and Master. Christ, early in His ministry, said to His disciples, "Come away by yourselves . . . and rest a while . . ." (Mark 6:31 NAS). There is a biblical principle clearly set forth regarding the need for rest. Christ is a perfect example. He never was in a hurry. It is not recorded that He ever ran. He walked. He prayed frequently, rested, and relaxed. At times, He removed himself from the crowds and disciples to be alone for rest and quiet relaxation. He truly is a model for us today.

The Apostle Paul encouraged those in the early church with these words, "And let us not lose heart in doing good, for in due time we shall reap if we do not grow weary" (Galatians 6:9 NAS). Again, to the church in Thessalonica he wrote, "But as for you, brethren, do not grow weary of doing good" (2 Thessalonians 3:13, NAS). These were important principles and guidelines for those living in the first century. They need to be heeded today more than ever.

Tom Mullen, in his delightful book, comments on this kind of life-style as it relates to today's world.

> To work too hard, too long, or too much is to take work too seriously. For those of us who are borderline workaholics, we need to develop the capacity to do nothing. This is not an easy task. Just getting untangled from having our eye on the ball, our ear to the ground, and our shoulder to the wheel will take considerable effort.[1]

In today's world, through the efforts of many scientists and social experts, we can readily see the effects of excessive work to the exclusion of leisure. No discussion is needed here. The physical, biological, and behavioral sciences show conclusively that there is a valid law of diminishing returns in our universe. Increased work produces the same effect. Production will begin to fall off at a certain point when a person overworks.

Gradually firms and workers are beginning to recognize the tremendous pressures of the day and are changing attitudes as well as work behavior to meet these stresses.

> In every society men perform the tasks, economic and non-economic, that fall to them by virtue of their social position. But the notion of "free time," time set aside and unconstrained, is a peculiarly modern idea; in the primitive tribe or peasant village, work is hardly distinguished from the rest of life—from the duties and rights as husband, son, father, clansman. Having conceived of the idea that time off work is free time, industrial man proceeds to define such time as one of the great benefits of economic growth.[2]

A national survey conducted by *Psychology Today* magazine shows that a new breed of worker is developing in America.[3] This new worker is beginning to make work less important and leisure more important. The survey indicated that only one in five individuals surveyed stated that work meant more to them than leisure. The majority (60 percent) said that while they enjoy their work, it was not their major source of fulfillment.

Many workaholics have no concept of just how uptight or tense they really are. Recognizably, one of the first ways to change this situation is to change the pattern of living. If workaholics are to enjoy leisure time they must learn or relearn some behavior patterns.

A Word About Stress

Leisure time serves a vital function in life because of outside pressures upon our lives. Authorities define stress as the reaction by the body to a stimulus that is unpleasant.

It should be made clear that we do not want to eliminate stress altogether. Many people work better when there is some type of stress. It is probably true that if there were no stress some people wouldn't even get up in the morning. Often people remark that they find stress very stimulating; it offers them a challenge. All workers must be aware that stress is a factor that must be dealt with in their daily lives on the job.

Doctors agree that a major cause of fatigue is more often mental than physical. Stress and depression are the prices that many people pay for surviving in today's complex and fast-changing society.

To a degree, everyone feels a mental strain in our contemporary world. Some people are vaguely aware that they feel blue most of the time. They lack the emotional energy to make new friends and enjoy special activities. They have a flat response to situations that stimulate other persons.

Dr. Lawrence E. Hinkle, Jr., of Cornell University's medical school, in a published newspaper report, believes that most people who suffer from lack of energy are fundamentally depressed. "They have trouble sleeping and trouble waking up," he said. "They have no drive or interest." [4]

Hinkle said that he finds energy-draining depression most common among adults who have worked hard and conscientiously toward a fixed goal for a long period of time. "We used to find this among mothers with small children and lots of domestic chores," he said. "Now we find it including the businessman who applies himself steadily, takes work home with him, and does not sleep well."

The body is a marvelous machine. It will usually signal when something is wrong. Heed its warnings and you will learn some very important things about yourself. The language of the body may help us to see what's behind that *workaholic* mask we may be wearing. Remember, anxiety and other emotions may cause a high percentage of physical symptoms known to medical science.

Dr. Hans Selye, noted expert on stress, is experimenting with ways to use stress to improve individual performance. He says that we use stress to grow with. It feels good and makes life exciting. Only the dead do not feel stress. It is his further view that the way a person reacts to a painful event—a death in the family or the breakup of a marriage—is more important than the event itself. He calls the energy that the body uses when it reacts to a stress situation "adaptation energy" and argues that it is a distinctly different type of energy than the kind people receive from food.[5]

One of the marks of a good worker is the appearance of ease with which he performs his duties. Have you noticed the workaholic? He seems always to be on the go, seeming to be continually out of breath. The person in a hurry often reveals that the thing he is tackling is too big for him.

Hurry and overwork are wearing on the body and nerves. No matter how high the pressure may be, it is well to frequently apply the brakes.

Too many workers have the idea that their irresistible drive demands that they ignore questions of health, leisure, and relaxation. They pay an exorbitant price, one that need not be exacted at all.

Only when the body is in good trim will the mind function at its highest efficiency. When his body is too tired to allow a man to read more than his evening paper, he is being deprived of mental sustenance in a way that will reflect itself in his work. When restlessness takes the place of directed activity, and a man begins to fidget, it may signify that he has been driving his machine too far, too fast. It's time to slow down.

The Child in Us

One way to slow down is to program into your life more leisure time, play time, if you please. The first step is to allow more time for it, and to get in touch with the child in yourself. Mature adults will often reject that part of their lives, believing that it is wrong to ever give themselves over to child-like thoughts, feelings, or behavior patterns.

Eric Berne's famous theory regarding human personality is known as Transactional Analysis ("TA"). He has presented to the world an interesting concept about the gamesmanship approach to problem solving with the adult human being a compendium of child, parent, and adult personalities. He says that there are at all times three ego states which constantly fall into basic categories of transactions with other human beings. By the time one is six to eight years old the script of life has been written into a cast of characters (adult, parent, and child) and the person spends the rest of life acting out the play. In various settings and under certain stimuli a person, through early learning, takes on one of these three states and gives off messages of self-sentences. The thoughts then trigger emotions.

The adult part represents the conscience, rationality, arbitration, and control part of us. The parent is the authority, dominance, and demand part. The child represents the reaction, emotion, and the fun and play part. If a person plays any one of these roles at inappropriate times, his life is ineffective. The idea in self-analysis is to take away any inappropriate models or responses to other persons.

It should be understood that the workaholic is a person who does not give enough time to being a *child*. It is certainly permissible at times to allow the child in us to surface. We've all known, for example, grown men who enjoy getting out the electric trains at Christmastime just as they did in their boyhood. There's nothing wrong with that.

Leisure or play is a basic ego state in all of us. To disallow it or inhibit its activity in adulthood is to miss a great part of life. The mature, balanced person has the freedom of choice to change at will from, say, the adult to the child. The *child* needs to be given more attention. When one is sensitive to the *child* in himself, he will also be more sensitive when he sees the *child* in others.

The workaholic needs to reflect on the truth that to become as a little child who can really play without any inhibitions is a great spiritual discovery and reality as well as a healthy psychological process in the personality.

If play is a basic need then people need to do it and do it well. Unfortunately, our contemporary culture has provided numerous blocks to play behavior, including authority messages, religious directives, and social expectations. We need to confront these blocks by developing a set of leisure values, assisting the person toward fulfillment, expression, and intimacy unrelated to work.

Play or leisure time also helps a person minimize his problems. After good hard play or involvement in some avocation, a person will often feel that his problems are not so difficult or imposing after all. Leisure helps one to keep things in perspective. To be able to turn away from the drab puritanism of work is a liberating experience. Being able to completely change pace provides renewal which brings one back to the simplicities of life.

Arnold Mandell, a San Diego doctor and noted author, has been the psychiatrist for the San Diego Chargers professional football team. He was a professed workaholic. It almost cost him his life, as he suffered a massive heart attack. He has turned his life around, still working hard, but now balancing it with pleasure. He has recently written of his experiences in a book entitled *After 35, a Journey Into the Second Cycle of Life.*[6]

After his heart attack he states that he lost his anchors in the workaholic world and had to struggle for a new meaning to life. He confesses that the power struggle in that world is greater than most imagine. One has to know his own limits, he says, and seek to discover what they are as well as the point at which one emotionally has to remove himself from the working environment.

He admits to learning a painful lesson. It is not the kind or the amount of work. Since all people are different, it is simply, he says, how people approach work.

Dr. Mandell almost paid the supreme sacrifice for his work attitudes. He learned in time the profound truth that the one-dimensional man is the one who has lost his freedom. He is only a part man.

Erich Fromm sees one of the basic needs for leisure as the change of pace it offers from the humdrum of everyday work. He advocates the cultivation of hobbies and free-time activities in contrast to the press-button services of automatic machines and the do-it-yourself activities.[7]

Learning to Relax

Learning the art—and it is an art—of relaxation is a vital key to relieving tension, whether it is spontaneous or planned. Do anything as long as it allows you to relax. It is important for all of us to seek variety or diversification from our regular routines.

For example, it probably wouldn't be best for a minister to read theological books in his leisure time, or for a person leading a sedentary life to take up chess, or for a nursery owner to plant a garden and care for it.

Variety is the key. Caress a pet, take a brief walk through the office corridor, read a magazine, go to the window and watch the cars below or an airplane above. It doesn't make much difference what you do, just break the cycle of tension.

It is also good to find periods each day devoted exclusively to relaxation. There are numerous mind-relaxing exercises which should be done daily. Anything that brings total-body relaxation and peace of mind will pay dividends. Quiet meditation or the development of spiritual, reflective techniques are effective relaxation methods.

Over the longer haul you might try to play an instrument,

learn some Chinese or Russian, memorize a book of the Bible.
Just employ a change of pace.

A number of techniques are offered to assist in relaxing.
Prayer or meditation is one of the best ways to be released
from tension. Leonard Cammer cites several other techniques.[8] Progressive relaxation was developed by Dr. Ed-
mund Jacobson for work-addicted executives in the 1930s. He
emphasized deep muscle relaxation. Autogenic training, de-
vised by Dr. Wolfgang Luthe, has begun to be an effective
technique. It emphasizes self-generated relaxation techniques
as a person concentrates to bring warmth and tranquility to the
body and mind.

Biofeedback is another technique by which to achieve relaxation. It monitors the tension and stress factors in the body.
One learns all kinds of emotional responses to stimuli in the
environment.

While We're at It . . .

Let's talk about vacations and holidays. Here's an interesting challenge for you. Examine the literature in the business
world on the subject. First, you'll notice a pitifully small
amount of copy devoted to the topic. Vacations are far too
often seen almost to be wrong because they are the opposite of
work. Note how some administrators look upon vacations as a
fringe benefit that is a burden to the organization.

However, changes for the better are increasingly taking
place. Changes in vacation and holiday practices continue to
be negotiated in collective bargaining. These become issues
because most labor unions express keen interest in some type
of extended paid vacations and a greater number of paid holidays. The four-day-workweek concept is gaining momentum
as well. For now, there remains greater interest in more paid
vacations and holidays to allow leisure time in our highly industrialized society.

Recognizing the value of vacations, companies like General
Motors now *require* all employees to take them. If there is
vacation time left over at the end of a given year, a person

cannot add that time to the next year's time. This encourages the employee to use up his entitled time.

It is recognized that a vacation does not necessarily have to be long in order to be therapeutic. Even one or two days off can be very beneficial in its effect, for it constitutes a refreshing change of pace.

Wayne Oates provides this helpful material about leisure and vacations:

> With the contemporary two-day weekend (an invention of the last few years), the pattern of official holidays, and the two-week to one-month vacation, the typical work year today looks something like this:
>
> 104 weekend days
>   7 special holidays
> 14 vacation days
> 125
> 16 extra days in the event of one-month vacations
> 141
> 224 working days
> 365 days a year
>
> The workaholic is living in an unreal world if he does not face up to the reality that one out of every three days is available for the meaningful use of leisure. While he should not tactically schedule every moment of leisure, he should have a conscious overall strategy that he has chosen. He should exercise his freedom from slavery by deciding for himself what the interruptions of work can mean. The crucial problem in the use of leisure is that the person has to decide for himself how to use his time. At work, it is usually decided for him. In this respect leisure calls for more independence than does work. It calls for more initiative and creativity. The work addict retreats into work rather than confront the insecurities and risks to be met in the world of play, repose, and unprogrammed contact with life itself.[9]

The Importance of Exercise

The key to improving personal vitality is no secret—planned exercise, a balanced diet, avoiding unnecessary stress, and diversifying one's life. Exercise is vital in helping to maintain a sound physical and emotional level in a person's life. Work often drains off so much energy that there are no reserves left to enjoy many of life's pleasures.

The problem is how to find those secrets for life's enjoyment while living in the workaday world. So often the office worker or executive, coming home from work, gets a pick-me-up cocktail or two and collapses in front of the TV set. Both are *no-no*'s in the personal energy game; alcohol depresses the central nervous system and only lifts the feeling of fatigue temporarily.

Studies on fatigue and energy disclose that some kind of physical activity, even if it's only a short walk, is infinitely better than slumping into an easy chair at the end of the workday.

Strenuous exercise is something else. You should consult a doctor before starting any extensive exercise program. Anyone who habitually feels exhausted should make an appointment for a complete medical examination, because fatigue is a possible signal of such serious illnesses as diabetes or heart disorders.

But to get started, mild exercise, if only for a few minutes a day, will enhance one's life immeasurably. Deep breathing, knee bends, and running in place for workers with sedentary jobs are helpful and therapeutic. (It may take a little imagination, though, to engage in such office exercises without causing the boss some consternation or provoking gibes from colleagues at work!) But remember, it's your life. It's no joke to be able to add years to your life by concerted effort.

Another effective office strategy is to use the coffee break time to exercise. It pays double dividends since too much coffee is not particularly helpful anyway.

All of these exercises increase your energy. Remember that the lack of exercise drains personal energy.

People who work hard and long hours are the ones who especially need some kind of physical activity. Such individuals may be compared with an automobile that is continually driven in the city, accumulating carbon in the engine. You've got to take the car out on the highway and drive it fast to clear out the engine.

A demanding schedule doesn't necessarily tire everyone. Some people thrive on nonstop challenges and they gather energy as they deal with one task after another. But for most, this is not the case.

Various authorities, in a magazine article, stated their views on exercise. "Exercise is one of the best ways to relieve the pressures caused by job stress," asserts Dr. George Williams, director of the Institute of Health Research in San Francisco. Donald W. Bowne, a medical director for Prudential Insurance, asserts that physical fitness serves as an inoculation against stress.

"The technique is completely unimportant," says Dr. Edward B. Mohns of the Scripps Clinic and Research Foundation in La Jolla, California. "I may run five or ten miles after work or listen to a Beethoven string quartet—and for 30 minutes I'm in a different place. I've switched gears."

But Michael Smith of the National Institute for Occupational Safety and Health warns: "If heavy physical exertion is not enjoyable, don't do it. Otherwise, you'll only create new tensions." [10]

Regardless of the exercise/relaxation method you use, it is amazing what a little exercise can do for the mind. For one thing, it helps to drain off built-up aggressiveness that may be bottled up. We've all had the exhilarating experience of feeling great after a brisk walk. A psychologist in England insists on his schizophrenic patients running. But, he insists that they run backward until they are completely physically exhausted! He contends that the reverse patterning of the brain, plus the physical aggressiveness, is extremely helpful in treating these individuals. In some patients, he reports remarkable success after only three weeks when they follow this program three times a day.

Most people, if they will try it, will find that they can rid themselves of tension by indulging in brief exercise. The famous transcendentalist, Ralph Waldo Emerson, admitted that when he became emotionally empty and intellectually dry, his writing ability diminished. To correct this, he would often take a short walk through his garden, hoe and weed and tend his flowers. This seemed to restore his creative drive.

In the end, everyone has to find his own best cure for job stress. As long as you find some means of exercising, you will build into your life a more effective way of finding relaxation to balance work pressures.

The chairman of the Bendix Corporation, William M. Agee, sums up the whole matter for us:

> When I started out in the business, I thought you had to devote your entire life to the job. And my life was all-consuming—all work and very little play. I now feel that you have to have a balanced personal portfolio. You have to have other interests. And those who don't, as a rule, tend to be under more stress, are less happy and less contented.[11]

Leisure time, relaxation, rest, vacations, a change of pace, recreation—they all contribute so profitably to our well-being. Don't miss these joys of a fulfilled and meaningful life. They provide that necessary balance which each of us needs to be all that God intended us to be.

13

An Effective Strategy—
The Balanced Life

One who can't decide what the important things in life are lets his life slip through his hands in little pieces.

HAVE you noticed the person who gets on a special kick? He suddenly gets an interest, say in boating or in stamp collecting. He becomes totally absorbed in this interest. Or, take people who become extremists about almost anything. Have you noticed how lopsided they can get? Try to get them for a moment on a different topic. Forget it. They will always, somehow, veer back to their favorite subject. Workaholics are much the same way. They're out of sync.

A solution for those caught in the work trap is to seek ways of changing their conditioned life-style so it will become more balanced. To do this, goals and priorities need to be set or readjusted.

One of the most important words in our English language is *balance*. Extremes or tangents in any area of our lives may well create confusion and distress. One of the basic keys the workaholic needs to find is balance in his living. In the Gospel of Luke, the Apostle, commenting about Jesus' childhood, wrote, "And Jesus increased in wisdom and stature, and in favour with God and man" (Luke 2:52).

Notice that Jesus dedicated His first years to living a healthy, balanced life. Physically, intellectually, emotionally, and spiritually there was growth because all levels of His life were integrated, thus, balanced. He combined all the basic elements needed for a disciplined and well-rounded life. He wants to do the same for us. Dr. John R. W. Stott states it plainly in his book, *Balanced Christianity:* "It seems that there is almost no pastime the devil enjoys more than tipping Christians off balance."

The workaholic is lopsided. He is overcommitted to one area of life. He overvalues work. He needs to overhaul his value system, his goals, and priorities.

The very nature of work today produces great imbalance in the living habits of many people. For example, we are seeing more and more of what might be called the "weekend marriage." Some husbands are so bound up with their work, including necessary travel for the company, that the only time for them and their wives to be together is the weekend.

The "weekend marriage" life-style is tied in with the American dream of career advancement. Couples need to learn to adjust to this not-so-good situation. There is much aloneness associated with this kind of arrangement, but an important key is to exert every effort to make the time that is spent together exciting and rewarding.

C. Peter McColough, Chairman of Xerox Corporation, states his position on the importance and need for balance:

> I look for breadth of interests. Individuals with broad interests are best able to perform within a company today. We face many societal changes, and the broad outlook and encompassing overview are more pertinent than the traditional, circumscribed career preparation . . . .
>
> I keep coming back to outside interests and their value in building corporate leaders. Here one doesn't lead and supervise because his or her name happens to be higher on the organizational chart. It's usually because of persuasiveness, character, personality or salesmanship. And that's the kind of leadership we want in the company . . . .
>
> Perhaps one of the most important qualities a man or

woman can possess is balance. That simply means one
doesn't go off the deep end. You balance your life with
wives, husbands, children, recreational activities, hobbies, physical programs and community involvement. To
go off in one area or another I think is a mistake and will
lead to trouble.[1]

How does a person get started toward a balanced life?
Dr. John Huffman, Jr., Pastor of St. Andrews Presbyterian
Church in Newport Beach, California, offers four steps which
may be helpful:

> One, we must sit down and prayerfully reflect on our
> lives. We must ask ourselves the questions: "Who am I?"
> "Why am I here?" "What is most important to me?" Life
> moves so rapidly today that we seldom find the time to
> reflect.
>
> Two, we must write down our primary purpose for liv-
> ing. What is it? Do I want to be worthy? Smart? Popular?
> Do I desire job security? A lovely home? A nice family?
> We must be honest with ourselves . . . . Do I want truly
> to glorify God and enjoy him forever?
>
> Three, we must ask ourselves: "What in my life is ex-
> cess baggage? What hinders me from achieving my pur-
> pose?"
>
> Four, we need to write down some specific goals . . . .
> There is a place for human initiative as we respond to
> what God has done for us. Do I have goals? Do I have
> intellectual, physical and spiritual goals? Do I have social
> goals?[2]

Do I Have Goals?

To attain a balanced life a person must have definite goals
for his living. Following are a number of goals which we have
emphasized for years in our time-management seminars
which have been held across the country.

Goal One: I will spend some time each day reading God's
Word and praying for myself as well as others. Ours is a day of
great activism. We recognize that good works are vital, but we

must not judge success simply by looking at external symbols of piety. Good deeds must issue from a deep devotion to God and our fellowman.

Goal Two: I will give my family a part of me in quality time each week. This includes dates with my wife and children, with time to talk and play, and not when I'm tired and have little to give, but when I'm refreshed.

Goal Three: I will see to it that my family and I spend time in our church as part of the worshipping community. I need other believers and they need me.

Goal Four: I will take time for myself in leisure, actually calendarizing events so that nothing else will come along and crowd out this necessary time.

Goal Five: I am going to give myself to others in some kind of service, either by sharing or by taking the time to be a friend with someone who may need me.

Goal Six: I will allow time for planning each week. This time will be utilized to constantly challenge my goals and my objectives, and to review my progress.

Goal Seven: I will serve diligently the job and employers who have hired me in good faith, fulfilling my responsibilities to the best of my ability.

You may want to include other goals or fill in more details on your stated goals. Whatever you do, be specific by naming the goals and by all means follow up the thoughts with action. Creating attainable and realistic goals is a vital element in leading a fulfilled, balanced life.

John Huffman says:

> Set short-range and long-range goals, realizing they are made to be broken. It is impossible to accomplish them all. However, we'll achieve more with goals drawn than we would without them. I must not live by accident, waiting for things to happen. I must make things happen . . . .
>
> People who are goal-oriented are the ones who achieve. There's a difference between having a purpose and having a goal. Purpose is a desire. A goal is setting up a prac-

tical measurement to see if I am accomplishing my purpose. Goals are goads. They goad us upward out of our
laziness, helping us to move forward. Do I have goals?
Goals will begin to organize us past that frustration of not
getting everything done that we want to do. We need
spiritual goals, social goals, and economic goals. Long-
range and short-range goals will allow us to measure our
progress in life.[3]

It is not enough to simply set our goals. We must continue to
challenge and analyze them. This is a vital necessity for a
well-rounded and meaningful life. It stands to reason if our
goals are not realistic or clear, we can't and won't know what
to work toward.

How Do I Spend My Time?

Another important factor in setting priorities is the management of our time. This has never been more vital than in
today's world where so many things vie for one's waking
hours.

Most executives work long and hard hours. Obviously some
people get more and better results in their work than others.
But there is no direct relationship that can be assumed between hard work and the level of performance. In fact, one
fallacy is that the man carrying his briefcase home is a symbol
of success. In many cases such an act may be the result of poor
management of time and the penalty of failure to plan
adequately.

Time management is crucial. People frequently get so en-
meshed in activity that they lose sight of why they are doing it.
The activity becomes the end in itself, a false goal. Successful
people do not lose sight of their goals and the hoped-for out-
puts. To be most effective, we must achieve maximum results
in minimum time.

Self-management, planning, organizing for maximum results, setting priorities, delegating, and action all fit into the
picture to attain maximum efficiency while one is on the job.

One of the best devices for overcoming the pressures of

work and for managing one's time is to have well-planned and documented calendars. This is what we call *calendarizing,* a great antidote for the disease of workaholism. Utilizing a planning calendar allows one to make provision in advance for planned evenings with the family, time for recreation, an evening set aside for reading, or a weekend away with the family.

A calendar, properly used and developed, can be the guiding light for allowing one the luxury of doing the things he really wants to do. Unless there is clear planning provided for by means of calendars, the things that we really want to do rarely happen.

It is also important to recognize that when calendarizing there is time over which we have no control. We must accept this fact. For example, there are the demands of our superiors at work, time to be given to our peers and subordinates, and emergencies which sometimes occur. But—way beyond this—there is far more *discretionary time* than one generally recognizes.

The time we have in this latter area may well be used creatively. We can't necessarily schedule times when we experience productivity, but we can strengthen our output (planning, writing, reading, and so forth) by scheduling some time to let the creative processes work.

The workaholic needs to have others help him with his calendar. He needs to confess the fact that this has been a problem to him and it is important to seek counsel from those who have already experienced these kinds of frustrations.

Where does time management really begin? How does a person make sure he will be successful in this area? A great deal has been written on this subject. When we boil it down, the answer falls into four basic categories.

1. Decide what it is that you want to do with your life. Set goals.
2. Establish priorities for the goals that you set.
3. Figure out how to reach these goals. This is planning.
4. Follow a procedure which will use the least amount of time to reach them. Schedule.[4]

And don't forget that *posteriorities* are extremely important as well. The setting of priorities is vital, but being selective in what we are *not* going to do is equally vital. It may be that the harder task is setting posteriorities and then sticking to the decision.[5]

It is important to recognize that the priorities we establish and set for ourselves are the result of the value system which we have established. Our value system is the reflection of our commitments and they are measured by what we are actually doing.

For the Christian, this value system should have its roots in the authority and instruction of the Word of God.

Since our situations will continue to be changing, it is important for us to review continually what we are doing and to see how it relates back to the Word of God.

There might be some broad basic principles that can help with this:

For the Christian, in our judgment, the broad levels of priorities in his value system are threefold, and the order here is very important.

First of all is our commitment to God in Christ. No Christian would argue with the fact that this has our highest priority and a recognition of this and a commitment completely to Christ takes care of many frustrations as far as pressures of time and life are concerned.

The second level of commitment is to the Body of Christ, to the church which He has raised up—His Bride. The Apostle Paul says in 1 Corinthians 12 that our body has many parts and the ear cannot say to the eye, "I have no need of you," or the foot cannot say to any other part of the body that it is unnecessary (*see* Verses 12–17). This relationship is a *given*, not a *choice*. All of us as Christians are stuck with each other; we do belong to each other.

In this second level of commitment to the Body of Christ we must recognize that our first priority, for those of us who are married, is to our spouse, then to our immediate family, and then to the extended family that God has given to all of us. Our measurement of Christian performance in this second commitment is our love for each other. The hallmark of the Christian is "Behold how they love one another" (*see* 1 John 3:23; John 13:34–35).

The third level of our priority commitment is to the work of Christ in the world, the task that God gives us to do. Far too often we confuse priority two with priority three, putting priority three ahead of two. This is where so often we face problems with the workaholic. He is not clear in his priorities.

Practically, in this whole matter of our personal priority planning, we need to work on our calendars and set goals for all of the levels of our commitments. For example, we all recognize the importance of our time with God—when we are consciously communing with Him through worship, prayer, meditation, and reading His Word.

We all recognize, again, although we don't always fulfill the recognition, the importance of our time with the family, when we are going to build into their lives and let them build into ours. We need dates to be made with husband or wife and with the children, to talk and to play. We need to have programs that strengthen our marriage and its goals and/or to make our spouse and children more effective.

We need time for ourselves, when we are going to have a relief valve for the pressures. This needs to be set aside in our daily calendar. Far too often we set goals to *use* ourselves, but we forget to set goals to *care* for ourselves. It is important to have these goals for ourselves for recreation—golfing, bowling, doing nothing, whatever fits our life-style.

Again, we need to have planned and scheduled time when we are going to be worshipping, praying, studying, or fellowshipping together. We need to take time for discipleship and building into the lives of others, whether it be the local church body or with cell groups, with couples or on a person-to-person level. It is important to schedule time for other people, time when we are going to be available for them and their goals.

The proper recognition of the importance of priorities in our daily living will help to allow us to have the time we really want to have to do the things we really want to do!

Prayerfully consider whether you really do believe that the priorities suggested above are operative in your life. Isn't God much more concerned with what you are than with what you accomplish, and isn't what you are demonstrated by the relationships that you have?

In essence, what the workaholic really needs in the matter of setting priorities is to seek a strategy for living. The Apostle Paul admonishes us to seek to live our lives with a keen sense of responsibility, not as men who do not know the purpose or meaning to life.

The late statesman Adlai Stevenson wrote, "It is not the days of your life, but the life in your days that counts." Timely words for those caught in the work trap.

Conclusion

ONE of the tragedies of life is that second chances seldom occur. Far too often we wait too long—until sickness, accidents, or calamities happen—before we make significant decisions or provide for changes to be made. Many die without ever enjoying the fullness of life because they lacked the courage to alter their life-style before some circumstance changed it for them.

For many workaholics, the addiction is not rectified before some deep conflict affects them. Others may stay at a job long after its challenge has passed. Because their priorities are twisted and perverted, most experience barrenness and unhappiness. Many suffer right up to their retirement, filled with cynicism and resentment caused by broken and hurt relationships—much of it due to their tackling an overabundance of work.

Let us summarize some positive approaches that may be taken to help insulate or immunize oneself from the *disease* of workaholism.

First, when a person is offered a position with a firm or an organization, he should not consider it unless he recognizes that he is qualified for it. Interviews do not always ascertain this information. The person himself knows deep down whether he has the tools, skill, and ability to function effectively in the job, thus giving him real satisfaction.

Second, a person should evaluate the basic reasons for considering a job. Is it money or power? Or is it to enhance creativity and provide fulfillment and satisfaction?

Third, a person should try to recognize what he can best offer his employer and not strive for positions that will dilute his effectiveness.

Fourth, a worker needs to constantly reassess his relationships away from the job, especially responsibilities to his immediate family.

Fifth, a worker must not be led by the value system of his wife or children who may seem to need prestige or creature comforts to make them happy.

Sixth, the worker needs to take a look at the bright side of life. If he can laugh at himself and his job conditions, this will relieve a great deal of tension.

For those with definite workaholic tendencies, the following summary steps may be helpful:

1. Have a thorough medical examination. Seek to determine if you are hypertensive. Take a treadmill heart test. A cardiovascular and gastrointestinal test will reveal a great deal about you.
2. Check—and recheck—your eating and exercise habits.
3. Get socially involved with friends. Calendarize some social events. Discuss your situation openly with your wife/husband or friends. Don't sit passively by, hoping things will happen. Do something; make things happen.
4. Reevaluate your vacation time, in light of your addiction. Don't take your briefcase along with you!
5. Make your problem known to others who may share the same difficulty. Perhaps you can emulate two executives who have worked out a buddy system. They check up on each other, making sure that the other does not become office-bound. They also plan social activities together. They chide one another if work becomes a topic for discussion.
6. If you get uptight over work because of a situation or individual, don't hide your feelings behind an empirical formula which closes all avenues of approach. Honestly express your feelings.
7. Develop a positive attitude concerning your work. Never forget that when used properly work remains one of the best therapies, and one of the best tranquilizers for a troubled spirit.

8. Evaluate your busyness on the job, which may not really be an integral part of it.
9. Plan some time alone each week to reflect and meditate about your life—its priorities and goals.

One of the special privileges in life is spending precious moments with those who love us dearly, our spouses, children, close friends. As we have seen, a characteristic problem of the workaholic is that he has misplaced values. In its acute form, he cannot fully enjoy those ecstatic moments which can never be recovered, such as celebrating an anniversary, sharing the great joy over the birth of a child, getting involved in a daughter's sweet-sixteen party, putting extra effort into a wedding in the family. Of such is the stuff of life.

Many workaholics find it extremely difficult to make prior commitments to these significant events. One thing is sure— you cannot substitute for them or send someone in your place. Missed opportunities will never again pass your way. The workaholic needs to adjust to the meaningful moments of his life and those whom he loves.

Hard work is good; consuming work is wrong. We must constantly guard against overwork that will deprive us of health, family, and a strong, effective spiritual life.

Learn to leave your work at work!

Remember, there is one fundamental basis for the disease of workaholism. If you want to keep your problems, work at them!

When you have been able to cut loose from the tyranny of excessive work, to be free at last to enlarge your horizons and become a greater part of your family and society, bear in mind that you will not want to slip back into the old patterns. Hopefully, those modes of doing and thinking will lose their meaning in light of the new behavior. One of the wonderful freedoms is that you no longer see yourself as indispensable. And, you will no longer be threatened by the thought of it.

In this book we have sought to indicate some corrective measures in facing the epidemic of what we have called workaholism. In summary, we have said that solutions may be found in such areas as:

Seeking spiritual renewal
Redefining success
Reassessing work satisfaction
Coping with stress
Learning to say no
Throwing off guilt
Getting close to those you love
Counseling with a professional as needed
Conditioning through exercise
Enjoying relaxation
Setting measurable personal, family, and work goals
Balancing a meaningful life-style
Scheduling leisure time for self and family
Prioritizing life's important issues
Establishing and maintaining an intimate walk with God
    through His Son, our Lord Jesus Christ

Finally, the future is yours. The philosopher-theologian Soren Kierkegaard said, "We can only understand life backwards but we can only really look forward." Life is like a kaleidoscope: the elements remain basically constant, only the pattern changes.

If you're caught in the work trap, you can be helped. You can change. You can be in charge of your life.

Keep work in its proper perspective and you will have a whole lifetime to rejoice over your labors. Angela Morgan's beautiful and moving poem epitomizes work as it should be, bringing delight and worth to the soul:

Work—A Song of Triumph

Work!
Thank God for the might of it,
The ardor, the urge, the delight of it—
Work that springs from the heart's desire,
Setting the brain and the soul on fire—

Oh, what is so good as the heat of it,
And what is so glad as the beat of it,
And what is so kind as the stern command,
Challenging brain and heart and hand?

Work!
Thank God for the pride of it,
For the beautiful, conquering tide of it,
Sweeping the life in its furious flood,
Thrilling the arteries, cleansing the blood,
Mastering stupor and dull despair,
Moving the dreamer to do and dare.
Oh, what is so good as the urge of it,
And what is so glad as the surge of it,
And what is so strong as the summons deep,
Rousing the torpid soul from sleep?

Work!
Thank God for the pace of it,
For the terrible, keen, swift race of it;
Fiery steeds in full control,
Nostrils a-quiver to greet the goal.
Work, the Power that drives behind,
Guiding the purposes, taming the mind,
Holding the runaway wishes back,
Reining the will to one steady track,
Speeding the energies faster, faster,
Triumphing over disaster.
Oh, what is so good as the pain of it,
And what is so great as the gain of it?
And what is so kind as the cruel goad,
Forcing us on through the rugged road?

Work!
Thank God for the swing of it,
For the clamoring, hammering ring of it,
Passion of labor daily hurled
On the mighty anvils of the world.

Oh, what is so fierce as the flame of it?
And what is so huge as the aim of it?
Thundering on through dearth and doubt,
Calling the plan of the Maker out.
Work, the Titan: Work, the friend,
Shaping the earth to a glorious end,
Draining the swamps and blasting the hills,
Doing whatever the Spirit wills—
Rending a continent apart,
To answer the dream of the Master heart.
Thank God for a world where none may shirk
Thank God for the splendor of work! [1]

ANGELA MORGAN

Appendix

Test for Suspected Workaholics

THE FOLLOWING TEST may be helpful to you or your friends in identifying the problem or level of work habits. Well-adjusted individuals or reasonably mature people will answer many of the questions the same way as a true workaholic. But the true workaholic will score much higher.

At the end of each statement place the appropriate number. Then total your score at the end.

Never	**Seldom**	**Occasionally**	**Often**	**Always**
0	**1**	**2**	**3**	**4**

1. I get uptight at work, so much so that I need something in my hand such as a cup of coffee, a pen, or a cigarette. _____
2. I find it difficult to relax. _____
3. There is a time urgency with me. _____
4. I constantly challenge others to produce more. _____
5. I worry over money and business. _____
6. I intentionally avoid people. _____
7. I am prone to wear myself out by undertaking too much. _____
8. I work under a great deal of tension. _____
9. I have a tendency to worry beyond reason over something that really does not matter that much. _____
10. Life is a strain for me much of the time. _____
11. There is an inclination in me to schedule more and more things into less and less time. _____
12. I have no spare time to myself. _____
13. I have difficulty in becoming involved in activities other than those related to my job. _____

14. I refrain from telephoning friends in the evening just to chat.
15. I prefer being a private person.
16. I stick to my principles, no matter what.
17. I get down on myself if I don't fulfill every one of my work obligations.
18. After completing a task, I review my work over and over again.
19. I'd rather be at work than most other places.
20. I am not as happy as others seem to be.
21. I find it hard to set aside a task that I have undertaken, even for a short time.
22. My job takes up most of my waking thoughts.
23. I prefer hard work which requires close attention, to work that allows me to be a bit careless.
24. I have a tendency to hide my true feelings.
25. I get "bent out of shape" if I am not punctual for appointments.
26. I do not let people finish what they say to me.
27. I prefer work outside the home to menial housework.
28. I bring work home from the job.
29. Doing nothing drives me up a wall.
30. I get annoyed when my spouse (or a friend) keeps me waiting.
31. I approach a hobby or sports with a *should* or *must* rather than with a *want to* attitude.
32. I get upset if I can't finish a work project that very day.
33. I have a tendency to measure work success in quantity rather than in quality.
34. I have periods when I lose sleep thinking about my job.
35. I have a strong compulsion to go to work on holidays or weekends.
36. I think that I work harder than most people on the job.
37. When I talk with someone my mind wanders to other subjects.
38. I have nervous gestures or tics.
39. I have difficulty delegating work to others.
40. I am more preoccupied with getting the things worth *having* than with the things worth *being*.

41. I find it difficult to develop love and companionship with my family. _____

42. I get upset if I have to wait in lines at banks, restaurants, and so forth. _____

43. When I get annoyed I have a tendency to keep it to myself. _____

44. Success to me is equated with hard work. _____

45. I find myself working when I could be relaxing. _____

46. I do things precisely to the last detail. _____

47. I worry about my performance on the job. _____

48. I would rather be admired by my co-workers than liked by my friends. _____

49. I am an intense person given little towards humor. _____

50. My spouse (or closest friend) thinks of me as a *workaholic*. _____

1. Now, **Total Up Your Score.** _____

2. If you answered questions 13, 17, 19, 22, 23, 32, 34, 35, 36, 39, 44, 45, 47, 48, and/or 49 with a 3 or 4 score, then add three points for each question thus marked. Place the points here. _____

3. Now, **Total Up the Two Scores.** _____

4. Find the corresponding total point score on the graph (next page) to determine the level of your attitudes and work habits. _____

WORKAHOLIC SCORING GRAPH

If you scored between 0–90 **Not a Workaholic** Keep up the good work!	*If you scored between 91–130* **Borderline Workaholic** Be careful.	*If you scored between 131–165* **Moderate Workaholic** Better reevaluate your life.	*If you scored above 165* **Compulsive Workaholic** Time to overhaul your life-style.

0 5 10 15 20 25 30 35 40 45 50 55 60 65 70 75 80 85 90 95 100 105 110 115 120 125 130 135 140 145 150 155 160 165 170 175 180 185 190 195 200

Source Notes

Chapter 1

1. Branislav Cukic, "Effects of Variations in Work Load." *Psihologije*, vol. 3, December, 1970, pp. 249–254.
2. S. M. Sales, "Effects of Variations in Work Load." *Dissertation Abstracts International*, vol. 30, October–December, 1969, p. 2407-B.
3. Wayne E. Oates, *Confessions of a Workaholic* (Nashville: Abingdon Press, 1971).
4. William H. Whyte, Jr., *The Organization Man* (New York: Doubleday, 1957).
5. Martin R. Haskell, *Socioanalysis: Self-Direction via Sociometry and Psychodrama* (Long Beach, Calif.: Role Training Associates of California, 1975).
6. Caroline Stevens, ". . . Eyedrops, Stress, Schizophrenia, More . . . ," *Working Woman*, III, no. 1 (January, 1978), p. 23.
7. Leland E. Hinsie and Robert J. Campbell, *Psychiatric Dictionary* (London: Oxford University Press, 1970), p. 15.
8. Oates, op. cit., p. 1.
9. Ted W. Engstrom, *The Making of a Christian Leader* (Grand Rapids: Zondervan Publishing House, 1976), pp. 117–18.
10. "Profiling the American Business Executive," *TWA Ambassador* (February, 1978), p. 13.
11. Alan N. Schoonmaker, *Anxiety and the Executive* (New York: American Management Association, Inc., 1969), pp. 66–67.
12. Oates, op. cit., p. 5.
13. Warren Boronson, "The Workaholic in You," *Money* (June, 1976), p. 33.
14. Peter S. Greenberg, "Work Addicts," *American Way* (December, 1977), p. 15.

Chapter 2

1. James C. Coleman and Constance L. Hammen, *Contemporary Psychology and Effective Behavior* (Glenview, Ill.: Scott, Foresman & Co., 1974), p. 341.
2. Lloyd Lofquist, *Adjustment to Work* (New York: Appleton-Century-Crofts, 1969), p. 7.
3. Ibid.

4. Ibid.
5. Sigmund Freud, *Civilization and Its Discontents* (*Das Unbehagen in der Kultur*, trans. Joan Riviere, Hogarth Press, 1930), p. 34.
6. Georges Friedmann, *The Anatomy of Work* (New York: Free Press of Glencoe, 1962), p. 127.
7. George Andrew Sargeant, "Motivation and Meaning." *Dissertation Abstracts International*, vol. 34, September–October, 1973, p. 1785-B.

Chapter 3

1. Raymond C. Baumhart, "How Ethical Are Businessmen?" *Harvard Business Review*, XXXIX (July–August, 1961), p. 172.

Chapter 4

1. Alan N. Schoonmaker, *Anxiety and the Executive* (New York: American Management Association, Inc., 1969), p. 29.
2. Leonard Cammer, *Freedom from Compulsion* (New York: Pocket Books, 1977), p. 34.
3. Ibid., p. 21.
4. Ibid., p. 27.
5. Meyer Friedman and Ray H. Rosenman, *Type A Behavior and Your Heart* (Greenwich, Conn.: Fawcett World Library, 1974), pp. 75–80.
6. Schoonmaker, op. cit., p. 49.
7. Oates, *Confessions*, pp. 22–23.
8. Ferdinand Zweig, *The British Worker* (London: Penguin Books, 1952), p. 97.
9. F. J. Roethlisberger, *Management and Morale* (Cambridge, Mass.: Harvard University Press, 1941), p. 24.
10. Theodore I. and Eleanor Rubin, *Compassion and Self-Hate* (New York: David McKay Co., Inc., 1975), pp. 175–176.
11. Erwin O. Smigel, *Work and Leisure* (New Haven, Conn.: College & University Press, 1963), pp. 171–172.
12. Jay Kesler, *I Want a Home With No Problems* (Grand Rapids: Zondervan Publishing House, 1978), pp. 39–40.

Chapter 5

1. Oates, *Confessions*, p. 13.
2. "Over Half of All Women Now Part of Job Market," *Santa Ana Register* (October 7, 1978).

3. Oates, op. cit., pp. 80–81.
4. Ibid., pp. 73–74.
5. Leonard Cammer, *Freedom*, pp. 31–32.
6. Ibid., p. 18.
7. Ibid., p. 20.
8. Ibid., p. 46.
9. Ibid., p. 89.
10. Oates, op. cit., p. 82.

Chapter 6

1. C. Peter Wagner, "Confessions of a Workaholic," *Eternity*, XXVI, no. 8 (August, 1975).
2. Ibid., p. 20.
3. Ibid., p. 25.
4. Bill L. Little, *This Will Drive You Sane* (Minneapolis: Comp Care Publications, 1977), pp. 96–97.
5. "I Was God's Workaholic," *Moody Monthly*, LXXVIII, no. 6 (February, 1978), pp. 85–87.

Chapter 7

1. John B. Miner, *The Management of Ineffective Performance* (New York: McGraw-Hill Book Co., Inc., 1963), p. 179.
2. Ibid.
3. David Macarov, *Incentives to Work* (San Francisco: Jossey-Bass, Inc., 1970), p. 71.
4. Ibid.
5. Oates, *Confessions*, p. 84.
6. Peter F. Drucker, "Big Business and National Purpose," *Harvard Business Review*, XL (March–April, 1962), pp. 49–59.
7. William H. Whyte, Jr., *The Organization Man* (New York: Doubleday, 1957).
8. Eugene E. Jennings, *The Mobile Manager* (Ann Arbor: University of Michigan Press, 1967), p. 96.

Chapter 8

1. Schoonmaker, *Anxiety*, pp. 130–131.
2. Ibid., p. 136.
3. R. D. Laing, *Politics of the Family* (New York: Random House, 1972), p. 98.
4. Schoonmaker, op. cit., p. 139.

5. Otto Fenichel, *The Psychoanalytic Theory of Neurosis* (New York: W. W. Norton & Co., 1972), p. 445.
6. Martin R. Haskell, *Socioanalysis: Self-Direction via Sociometry and Psychodrama* (Long Beach, Calif.: Role Training Associates of California, 1975), p. 25.
7. Ibid., p. 38.
8. Fenichel, op. cit., p. 298.
9. Oates, *Confessions*, p. 25.
10. Karl Menninger, *Love Against Hate* (New York: Harcourt, Brace & World, Inc., 1970), pp. 161–162.
11. Oates, op. cit., p. 88.
12. Fenichel, op. cit., pp. 472–473.

Chapter 9

1. Cammer, *Freedom*, p. 7.
2. Karl Menninger, *Love Against Hate* (New York: Harcourt, Brace & World, Inc., 1970), p. 143.
3. Ibid.
4. Schoonmaker, *Anxiety*, pp. 52–53.
5. Meyer Friedman and Ray H. Rosenman, *Type A Behavior and Your Heart* (Greenwich, Conn.: Fawcett World Library, 1974), p. 192.
6. Theodore I. and Eleanor Rubin, *Compassion and Self-Hate* (New York: David McKay Co., Inc., 1975), pp. 133–134.
7. Schoonmaker, op. cit., p. 249.

Chapter 10

1. Albert Ellis and Robert A. Harper, *Guide to Rational Living* (North Hollywood, Calif.: Wilshire Book Co., 1966), p. 154.
2. Ibid., pp. 155–156.
3. Gary Collins, *You Can Profit From Stress* (Santa Ana, Calif.: Vision House Publishers, 1977), pp. 119–120.
4. "Professional Burnout—and How to Avoid It," *Family Weekly* magazine, *Santa Ana Register*, February 12, 1978, p. 30.
5. Ted W. Engstrom, *The Making of a Christian Leader* (Grand Rapids: Zondervan Publishing House, 1976), p. 165.

Chapter 11

1. Milton Rockmore, "Management Shopping List," *American Way* (American Airlines), October, 1977.
2. Philip G. Zimbardo, *Shyness* (New York: Jove Publications, Inc., 1977), pp. 209–10.

3. Ibid.
4. Ibid.
5. Ibid.
6. Ibid.
7. Ibid.
8. Ibid.
9. Cammer, *Freedom*, pp. 195–196.

Chapter 12

1. Tom Mullen, *Seriously, Life Is a Laughing Matter* (Waco: Word Books, 1978), p. 40.
2. Erwin O. Smigel, *Work and Leisure* (New Haven, Conn.: College and University Press, 1963), p. 123.
3. Daniel Yankelovich, "The New Psychological Contracts at Work," *Psychology Today* (May, 1978), p. 49.
4. "Jobs, Diet, Stress, Lack of Exercise Drain Personal Energy," *Santa Ana Register* (January 22, 1978), p. A–13.
5. Hans Selye, "Stress," *The Rotarian*, 132, no. 3 (March 1978), p. 20.
6. Arnold Mandell, *After 35, a Journey Into the Second Cycle of Life* (New York: Summit Books).
7. Erich Fromm, *The Sane Society* (New York: Holt, Rinehart & Winston, 1955).
8. Cammer, *Freedom*, pp. 215–219.
9. Oates, *Confessions*, p. 44.
10. *U.S. News & World Report*, "Stress," p. 81.
11. Ibid.

Chapter 13

1. Milton Rockmore, "Management Shopping List," *American Way* (American Airlines), October, 1977.
2. John A. Huffman, Jr., *Growing Toward Wholeness* (Waco: Word Books, 1978), pp. 18–19.
3. Ibid., pp. 20, 84.
4. Ted W. Engstrom and Edward R. Dayton, *The Art of Management for Christian Leaders* (Waco: Word Books, 1976), p. 213.
5. Ibid., p. 214.

Conclusion

1. Joseph Morris and St. Clair Adams, comps., *It Can Be Done: Poems of Inspiration* (New York: George Sully & Company, 1921), pp. 18–19.

Bibliography

Baumhart, Raymond C. "How Ethical Are Businessmen?" *Harvard Business Review*, XXXIX, July–August, 1961, p. 172.

Boronson, Warren. "The Workaholic in You." *Money*, June 1976, p. 33.

Cammer, Leonard. *Freedom From Compulsion*. New York: Pocket Books, 1977.

Coleman, James C., and Hammen, Constance L. *Contemporary Psychology and Effective Behavior*. Glenview, Ill.: Scott, Foresman & Co., 1974.

Collins, Gary. *You Can Profit From Stress*. Santa Ana, Calif.: Vision House Publishers, 1977.

Cukic, Bransislav. "Effects of Variations in Work Load." *Psihologije*, vol. 3, December, 1970, pp. 249–254.

Drucker, Peter F. "Big Business and National Purpose." *Harvard Business Review*, XL, March–April, 1962, pp. 49–59.

Ellis, Albert, and Harper, Robert A. *A New Guide to Rational Living*. North Hollywood, Calif.: Wilshire Book Co., 1966.

Engstrom, Ted W. *The Making of a Christian Leader*. Grand Rapids: Zondervan Publishing House, 1976.

————, and Dayton, Edward R. *The Art of Management for Christian Leaders*. Waco: Word Books, 1976.

Fenichel, Otto. *The Psychoanalytic Theory of Neurosis*. New York: W. W. Norton & Co., 1972.

Freud, Sigmund. *Civilization and Its Discontents (Das Unbehagen in der Kultur)*. Hogarth Press, 1930.

Friedman, Meyer, and Rosenman, Ray H. *Type A Behavior and Your Heart*. Greenwich, Conn.: Fawcett World Library, 1974.

Friedmann, Georges. *The Anatomy of Work*. New York: Free Press of Glencoe, 1962.

Fromm, Erich. *The Sane Society*. New York: Holt, Rinehart & Winston, 1955.

Greenberg, Peter S. "Work Addicts." *American Way*, American Airlines, December 1977, p. 15.

Haskell, Martin R. *Socioanalysis: Self-Direction via Sociometry and Psychodrama*. Long Beach, Calif.: Role Training Associates of California, 1975.

Hinsie, Leland E., and Campbell, Robert J. *Psychiatric Dictionary*. London: Oxford University Press, 1970.

Huffman, John A., Jr. *Growing Toward Wholeness*. Waco: Word Books, 1978.

"I Was God's Workaholic." *Moody Monthly*, LXXVIII, no. 6, February 1978, pp. 85–87.

Jennings, Eugene E. *The Mobile Manager*. Ann Arbor: University of Michigan Press, 1967.

Kesler, Jay. *I Want a Home With No Problems*. Grand Rapids: Zondervan Publishing House, 1978.

Laing, R. D. *The Politics of the Family*. New York: Random House, 1972.

Little, Bill L. *This Will Drive You Sane*. Minneapolis: Comp Care Publications, 1977.

Lofquist, Lloyd H., and Dawis, Rene V. *Adjustment to Work*. New York: Appleton-Century-Crofts, 1969.

Macarov, David. *Incentives to Work*. San Francisco: Jossey-Bass, Inc., 1970.

Mandell, Arnold. *After 35, A Journey Into the Second Cycle of Life*. New York: Summit Books.

Menninger, Karl. *Love Against Hate*. New York: Harcourt, Brace & World, Inc., 1970.

Miner, John B. *The Management of Ineffective Performance*. New York: McGraw-Hill Book Co., Inc., 1963.

Morris, Joseph, and Adams, St. Clair, comps. *It Can Be Done: Poems of Inspiration*. New York: George Sully & Company, 1921.

Mullen, Tom. *Seriously, Life Is a Laughing Matter*. Waco: Word Books, 1978.

Oates, Wayne E. *Confessions of a Workaholic*. Nashville: Abingdon Press, 1972.

"Profiling the American Business Executive." *TWA Ambassador*, Trans World Airlines, February 1978, p. 13.

Rockmore, Milton. "Management Shopping List." *American Way,* American Airlines, October 1977.

Roethlisberger, F. J. *Management and Morale.* Cambridge, Mass.: Harvard University Press, 1941.

Rubin, Theodore I., and Eleanor. *Compassion and Self-Hate.* New York: David McKay Co., Inc., 1975.

Sales, S. M. "Effects of Variations in Work Load." *Dissertation Abstracts International,* vol. 30, October–December, 1969, p. 2407–B.

Santa Ana Register. "Professional Burnout—and How to Avoid It," 12 February, 1978, p. 30.

Santa Ana Register. "Jobs, Diet, Stress, Lack of Exercise Drain Personal Energy," 22 January 1978, p. A–13.

Santa Ana Register. "Over Half of All Women Now Part of Job Market," 7 October 1978.

Sargeant, George Andrew. "Motivation and Meaning." *Dissertation Abstracts International,* vol. 34, September–October, 1973, p. 1785–B.

Schoonmaker, Alan N. *Anxiety and the Executive.* New York: American Management Association, Inc., 1969.

Selye, Hans. "Stress." *The Rotarian,* CXXXII, no. 3, March 1978, p. 20.

Smigel, Erwin O. *Work and Leisure.* New Haven, Conn.: College & University Press, 1963.

Stevens, Caroline. ". . . Eyedrops, Stress, Schizophrenia, More . . . ." *Working Woman,* III, no. 1, January 1978, p. 23.

U.S. News & World Report. "How to Deal With Stress on the Job," March 13, 1978, pp. 80–81.

Wagner, C. Peter. "Confessions of a Workaholic." *Eternity,* XXVI, no. 8, August 1975, p. 19.

Whyte, William H., Jr. *The Organization Man.* New York: Doubleday, 1957.

Yankelovich, Daniel. "The New Psychological Contracts at Work." *Psychology Today,* vols. 11, 12. May 1978, p. 49.

Zimbardo, Philip G. *Shyness.* New York: Jove Publications, Inc., 1977.

Zweig, Ferdinand. *The British Worker.* London: Penguin Books, 1952.

Index

219